THE GLORY YEARS

For Louise,
Emerald, Coco
and my grandchildren

THE GLORY YEARS

More Chapters of Accidents

THEO FENNELL

MENSCH PUBLISHING

Mensch Publishing
51 Northchurch Road,
London N1 4EE, United Kingdom

First published in Great Britain 2025

A catalogue record for this book is
available from the British Library

ISBN: HB: 978-1-912914-79-1 eBook: 978-1-912914-80-7

Typeset by Van-garde Imagery, Inc., • van-garde.com

Contents

PREAMBLE

Much to my own and many of my friends' surprise, I was asked to write another volume of 'Chapters of Accidents'.

The first volume, *I Fear for This Boy*, took its title from my final school report, so originally I thought I might as well use yet another disappointing comment, this time from my economics master's report, as the title for the second volume.

Why I was doing economics at A level is still a mystery to me and can only have been because the reading list was shorter than, say, history. In retrospect it seems ironic that I should have even contemplated a subject that I have since spent a lifetime paying no attention to, not even its most basic precepts.

The long-suffering master who tried to teach me, whose sighs and eye rolling whenever I tried to be amusing I can still remember, also wrote but a single sentence as his final report. He cleverly employed both an economy of words and an economist's expression.

'Your son's Economics work shows a very poor return on your investment.'

But, having decided on 'A Poor Return' as the title, a rather earnest person was asking me about my first book which they had recently read. They were congratulating me, without a hint of irony, on having the strength of character to have got through my terrible youth that they had interpreted as fraught and dangerous. When they asked me, after such a troubled start in life, what the second book was to be called, I couldn't resist.

'Volume two,' I answered, '*The Glory Years*.'

'Oh, good,' they answered sweetly. 'So glad things got better.'

They didn't. So, here follows, *The Glory Years: More Chapters of Accidents*.

1

GOING JAPANESE

For some time, in the 1980s and 90s, my company was featured in a very prominent and successful chain of Japanese department stores whose flagship store was in Tokyo.

The request to join them had come out of the blue from a very neat and smiling young man who spoke beautiful, if old-fashioned, English. He appeared one day in the small shop we then had in London on the corner of the Fulham Road, having seen our work in Harrods where we had recently opened a small concession.

I really knew nothing of Japan or of the Japanese and their ways but asking around, in those pre-internet days, I was assured that the company he represented was the best in its field and had been retailers since the 17th century.

After we had agreed that they would carry our work, we discussed what he wanted from us and it appeared to be our sterling silver models of cars, boats and anything else that a Japanese businessman might give as a present to another Japanese businessman as, in those days, giving each other original and expensive presents was a prerequisite of two titans doing business together.

We did, and still do, pride ourselves on the skill and detail of our model making and especially on being able to reproduce, in silver or gold, the wildest flights of fancy in miniature.

He also wanted our jewellery, the more unusual the better as those Japanese who weren't deeply conservative were very avant garde.

The sort of thing a Japanese businessman might give to a Japanese businesswoman or, indeed, his wife.

To start with they were to have the sole rights to our work in Japan for three years. They would place a sizable, initial order and then they would replenish every sale and spend a minimum every year. A part of this deal was that I was to go over to Tokyo twice a year for a week to host a show and be there for any other sales and marketing initiatives they thought might work.

Later I would go on a couple of these trips with Bruce, who worked with me and had the ability to make me laugh inappropriately more than anyone alive. These turned out to be a very bad idea in a land where any inappropriate laughter is viewed as an insult of the very worst kind.

My first trip was, however, solo and so I began to ask around for hints about the mores, habits, likes and dislikes of the Japanese so as not to cause any unconscious offence.

In those days, all Tokyo businessmen dressed in a uniform of black suits, white shirts and ties with the women togged out much the same but sometimes minus a tie. There would be a few people dressed in their wonderful traditional outfits and, outside Tokyo, people of the soil dressed as they might have in Hokusai's day.

I was told that their complicated and unbreakable etiquette was to be rigorously followed and that I should bow as often as possible, learn to sit cross-legged, never to tell a joke and whatever happened, never make anyone feel foolish or appear to be rude.

Apart from the cross-legged sitting it seemed it was going to be almost impossible for me to follow.

There being few Japanese restaurants in Britain then and no internet, the best information I could find was a guidebook that had been written in the sixties and had pictures of terrifying looking food and unsmiling, enigmatic people.

An unreliable friend of mine cheered me up a bit by telling me that Japanese women found tall, blond men irresistible and that I would be mobbed wherever I went.

The counterpoint to this came from a more reliable friend who told me that tall men, especially blond ones, were considered to be the devil incarnate and that Japanese ladies would probably throw things at me and then run and hide, perhaps for years, if they so much as caught a glimpse of me.

So, I had no real training for my first trip and, apart from this contradictory information, nor did I take enough trouble to seek any. I believed that I had seen enough of the world, having even lived in the far east, to be able to take Japan as it came. After all, how different can two peoples be as we are each of us humans?

Very, it turned out.

My first taste of a clash of cultures came when I visited customs at Tokyo airport to present my paperwork for the jewellery I had brought with me for the show I was to give at my sponsor's flagship store. When I opened my briefcase, the eagle-eyed young officer spied the edge of a magazine sticking out from behind one of the flaps inside its lid.

He pointed at this and I explained that it was a magazine, in a rather patronising, loud and slow voice; I had been told that very few Japanese spoke English which was true in those days.

He motioned me to take it out.

It was a copy of *Playboy* I had bought at the airport to read all its interesting articles on the plane, obviously.

If it had been a kilo of cocaine, it couldn't have elicited a more fevered reaction.

He immediately and theatrically donned some latex gloves, picked up the magazine as if it were a live snake, opened it to a page showing a naked woman, held it above his head and blew a whistle.

At first I thought I might be part of one of those rather cruel, television game-shows beloved of the Japanese, the object of which

3

is to humiliate someone so that they fear life forever more. But no, he plucked at my shoulder, closed my briefcase and marched me across the airport waving the offending periodical.

I was a good foot taller than everyone else, it seemed, and my clothes, though not particularly ostentatious by Western standards, looked positively exuberant among the universal black and white of Japan in those days.

It was difficult to know how to behave in this situation. Was an insouciant half-smile and casual amble the right approach or perhaps a slightly embarrassed eye-rolling at the silliness of it all?

Neither was the answer.

The young man was determined to deliver me to the guards housed in a small room with a glass front and he did so loudly and without ever smiling.

The open nature of this police room magnified my embarrassment as the senior of the two officials quizzed me for nearly half an hour about my reasons for having pornography about my person.

This seemed to be carried out in loud and barely decipherable English, but I was soon to learn that any interview, whatever the reason, always appeared to be an inquisition.

During this interrogation, he held up every offending page he found for the substantial crowd outside this glass box to view.

'Yooooooou like?!' he goaded me.

It was difficult to answer these questions as a yes would prove me a pervert and a no might prove worse.

I tried to explain to him and his cohorts, one of whom spoke good English, that the quality of the writing and the fascinating interview with some American quarterback were the real reasons for my having the magazine, but it was no good.

After a lengthy and incomprehensible harangue, he finally put the publication in a paper bag, sealed it and made me sign across the flap. I tried to tell him to keep it or throw it away, but he was set on his course, and I could see the glint of resolve through his round spectacles.

After this unfortunate turn of events, I had to get him to sign my customs papers and fetch my suitcase while many of my co-travellers regarded me with deep suspicion.

I realised I had, by now, kept the person sent to meet me waiting so, as I collected my luggage, I was inventing an excuse. Before it could take shape, a bland-looking man in glasses and a suit at least two sizes too big for him introduced himself.

'Theo San?' He asked, bowing and taking my suitcase.

'Yes, and who are you?' I replied.

'I am Mr Kola, your guide and to translate.'

'Aha, great stuff. Sorry I'm late, I got caught up at customs.' I said in as business-like a manner as I knew how.

'A lot of paperwork....customs, many papers.' I added.

'Yes, but no problem, we get your pornomag when you leave.' He answered with a sly grin.

As we got into the smart black saloon with a bald and angry-looking driver, I realised that, though I had discovered the Japanese word 'pornomag', I had lost much gravitas and would need to appear more professional before I could build a relationship with Mr Kola.

The hotel, when we finally arrived through the dense and turgid traffic, turned out to be owned by my sponsors as was almost every organisation, restaurant, golf course and shop we visited.

My room was unbelievably clean but not built for someone my size and, as it always did during my early visits there, everything made me feel vast and bovine.

The bed was on the floor, the bath was configured in a way that made no sense to me and the lavatory had me utterly beaten until I discovered that you sat back to front on it. I have never rendered myself so spotlessly clean as I did during those first few visits to Tokyo.

After my battle with the bathroom, I decided to go downstairs and wander about central Tokyo a bit.

Outside my door, sitting patiently on a chair, was Mr Kola. I was to learn that this is where he spent much of his off time.

Being at my beck and call, as I was an honoured guest, was the reason he gave initially but, as I got to know him better, he admitted that he was as much a guard as anything else, to make sure I wasn't poached by another company or did anything that might bring the business he worked for, and had dedicated his life to, into disrepute.

He need never have worried on the poaching front, but the second reason was fair enough.

I asked him what he did to amuse himself in Tokyo and he looked at me blankly. This seemed to be a foreign concept and I learned, over my time spent with Mr Kola, that it was.

Whiskey and Karaoke were his two weekend releases, he told me, but he was certainly not going to dabble in either in my solitary company as the loss of face would have been too great. I tried to explain that I was sure I would lose face in front of him at some point – a prediction which turned out to be bang on any number of times - so why didn't we lose face together and we could be quits? But it turned out the system didn't work quite like that.

Everyone in this revered and ancient company was delightful to me and at huge pains to show me the very best of Japan's extraordinary culture but I worked out that they needed to get the measure of me to see, as it were, where they could and couldn't take me.

So, I had to wait a few days to sample the heady delights of Tokyo nightlife and then in the company of the Chairman of the company who I only ever knew as Kakka, meaning my Lord, or some such thing, a form of address I'd picked up somewhere. It delighted him for obvious reasons and me for reasons undreamt of by him.

It is hard to overstate how important and influential the chairman of a huge Japanese company was in those days and might still be for all I know.

In a traditionally highly stratified society like Japan's, used to an Emperor and a ruling caste for centuries, something had to take its place after the war. For a time, the Americans were their *de facto* rulers but, when they left, the country began to slide back and away from the brashness of their system to readopt their more traditional ancient mores. This made captains of industry and chairmen of great boards the new aristocrats and they wielded enormous power. As the places we went to were all owned by his own company, the chairman was treated as one step below divinity.

This was neither very helpful in a business sense, as for reasons of fairness he didn't want to be seen to favour me, or in a social sense as there was little he wanted to do when first we met, in the way of entertainment, that set my pulse racing.

I should explain that Kakka was very old, a respected and much-admired statesman in Japan, and I was then probably forty years his junior. He was small, even by the standards of his contemporaries, and had a bald, slightly flaking pate with rheumy eyes, half-hidden behind very thick round spectacles of the sort the National Health used to dole out to boys like Piggy in *Lord of the Flies*.

His lack of outward vigour betrayed his exalted and powerful status but, when he gave a subordinate – and often quite a senior one – a wigging, out of hearing of his contemporaries but within mine, they became terrified, shaking with quivering bottom lips in a way that looked like it might even herald a loss of bladder control.

I realised he was tough to the very core and had probably seen things it was better only to guess at as the war, in which he must have taken part, was a completely forbidden subject.

After a few meetings, he began to trust me more than I deserved and to realise that, though I enjoyed Sumo wrestling, Kabuki theatre and blossom in small doses, I was never going to become completely captivated by any of them.

This left the door open for him to suggest some alternative, recherché local delights, not all of which I embraced fully.

This was at a time when virtually no Japanese spoke English, when nothing was printed or displayed in any other language than theirs and there were no mobile telephones. Making yourself understood was very difficult and tall, European men were looked on either as idiotic barbarians or with a sense of distaste for their lack of refinement.

This aversion extended to almost every local woman. As I said, I had been told by one source that they would be in awe and romantic thrall to a tall, blond westerner but my second source proved to be on the money as they either shied away in terror when I approached or burst into fits of laughter.

My only way of communicating, other than sign language, was through Mr Kola whose English was lamentable but which I had to pretend, for his sake, was fluent. So, as he was my only permanent colleague and I needed his discretion, I made intelligent faces and noises whenever he translated for me.

Sometimes Kakka and I spent evenings sampling the strange, local eateries alone, which was complicated as neither of us really understood the other, but these forays were filled with almost permanent and inexplicable laughter.

The first of our dinners out, Kola was with us, and it established a precedent that I came to fear even more than most of the earlier cultural excursions.

First, we would go to a restaurant of his choice, always one owned by the company and always very high-end and traditional cuisine. Those absurd dishes you might read about - the kind where the gall bladder from a sperm whale has been cut out with a sword and coddled with hummingbird tongues for twelve years - were regularly laid before me, night after night.

As I asked what each terrifying looking dish contained, Mr Kola attempted to describe, in his slight English, things for which there are no words in English – or indeed most other languages – the object in question being so obscure that no word was ever deemed necessary.

I felt for him but, in many ways, it helped to be oblivious to what I was eating, as the dishes mainly consisted of things dredged up from the very bottom of the sea, as yet unknown to man until a few days previously, mixed with other, nameless horrors of the deep and often served raw.

These culinary outrages were delivered to the table by a quivering and sad-looking geisha, her eyes not surprisingly averted from the devil's fare she had silently delivered as she knelt by the table.

I wondered what these poor women thought of the huge bloke, obviously struggling to sit on the floor under the low table, so ill at ease and looking less well after each course.

I always tried to eat as much as I could to be polite, but my feigned delight and Mr Kola's lack of vocabulary when he was there, were often my downfall.

At our first dinner, a very beautiful and delicately made little pot arrived in front of me with much more than the usual fanfare.

I lifted the lid and peeped inside.

I was appalled by what I saw.

In a gloopy, dark liquid, something was most definitely still moving. I looked apprehensively at Kola and he, in turn, spoke to Kakka.

His explanation, from what I understood of it, was that this thing was a live sea-creature, suspended in some sort of obscure albumen, mixed with other untranslatable horrors. The sporting thing about this particular creature, it transpired, was that it was highly toxic for most of its life cycle but, at this very special time of year, could be eaten with little risk.

Hurrah, I thought, but then I mused, why would you do that, unless it had some unbelievable healing properties or induced an erection of heroic proportions?

Nothing could conceivably taste that good but, perhaps, if you were in advanced old age, like Kakka, the stakes were not quite so high.

He grinned at me as I looked to him for guidance.

As usual, I couldn't work out whether this scenario was meant to be a gentle humiliation or a sign of his generous friendship.

He picked up his bowl, took off the lid and, with one theatrical move, swallowed the contents in a single gulp, as you might a raw egg. Then he rolled his eyes in a way that was unnervingly orgasmic while making little puffing noises. Then, after a few seconds, he let out a huge and noisy sigh.

Kola and the geishas smiled broadly and clapped....what on earth?

I picked up my little pot, took off the top and looked apprehensively into the darkness. Whatever it was moved in a turgid but threatening way in its bed of slime and my throat clenched.

But then I thought, it only took a few seconds and Kakka seemed to enjoy it.

The first sensation was immediate and repulsive, the concoction smelt of that part of any international dockside where the bilge from every ship and the waste from every sailor collects before it washes out to sea, and it hit my nostrils like a slap.

With my eyes watering, I put the rim of the pot to my lips and threw the contents, which turned out to be a sea-anemone, into my mouth hoping that the whole concoction would disappear straight down to my belly.

The liquid, viscous and foul though it was, did just this but the sea- creature simply got as far as the back of my throat and clung on there like its cousin, the limpet.

My body convulsed at this unexpected invasion and my gag-reflexes didn't reflex at all. I desperately worked it back into the cavity of my mouth, noting out of the corner of my eye the mounting hilarity of those staring open-eyed at my discomfort. I started to make plaintive little noises as my tongue tried to find ways to dislodge the brute.

In an act of bravado and desperation I bit down into the clinging polyp.

This was a mistake.

Suddenly the tang of all the terrors that lurk under the ocean wave and the gut-heaving taste of every revolting slimy, self-procreating creature of the deep exploded into my mouth.

I let out a succession of loud roars and inhuman grunts which seemed to amuse my Japanese friends even more.

As I shook my head and turned my neck, trying to force the blighter down me, the room became a madhouse with the small audience slapping their thighs and behaving in a way I never suspected possible from such introverted people.

I was to come to realise that the Japanese, once loosened by alcohol and farcical behaviour, lost all inhibition.

I stood up, hoping that gravity would lend a hand and a bowing, shuffling Geisha handed me a flask of sake and a little cup, averting her eyes from this enormous oaf and his terrifying convulsions.

I declined the cup and put the flask to my mouth, gulping down the sake as if it were water and, to my intense relief the creature began to slide slowly down my gullet.

The relief was instantaneous, as was the effect of nearly a pint of sake and these two sensations mingled to make me feel that all was right with the world again and that I was at one with my fellow men. This was in the mistaken belief that, although I was the cause of their mirth, they were laughing with me not at me.

As I learnt, the more I travelled to that excellent country, I couldn't have been more wrong. I was almost always an object of comical derision and, once I understood that, I began to enjoy my role as the unintentional jester.

We finished dinner with a cold and slightly scented pudding that went some of the way, along with more bucketsful of sake, to dispel the lingering, evil taste. At that stage, I hadn't learnt to respect sake, believing it to be a mild, amateur's drink and found myself very much drunker than I had expected.

Kakka now had the bit between his old yellow teeth and was determined to make a night of it. We crowded out of the restaurant into a novel and luxurious minibus with much bowing and scraping from strangers on the pavement. It was astonishing how much respect and servility this ancient man, in effect merely the chairman of a chain of department stores, elicited.

Our next stop was a karaoke bar.

Now a staple of every city, in the 1980s this was a new concept and hadn't yet made it to the West. I was more than familiar with the joys of a sing-song and even of miming while air-guitaring to a record, indeed, I would say I was an *aficionado* of both these great arts, but I had never seen the genius idea of karaoke in practice.

Again, people bowed and scraped as we entered an extra-ordinarily kitsch hall, unlike anything I had seen so far in Tokyo, with bright fair-ground lights flashing and a sort of 1950s, American hick-town vibe.

Someone was singing Rod Stewart's anthem, *Sailing*, to a superb backing track but in an appalling and tuneless voice with the words only recognisable in patches and, hearing it really badly done, I began to grasp the comedic brilliance and potential of karaoke.

Amazingly, the packed crowd were waving and swaying to this screeching rendition with the same, drunken sentimentality of a Scottish crowd in front of Sir Rodney himself.

Drinks were brought over to our table, without us even asking, which turned out to be heady brews of Southern Comfort, Suntory whiskey and lemonade, apparently a favourite thirst-quencher for the more dedicated participants.

An elegant lady with a book of song choices appeared from nowhere bowing to us both. She was in charge of taking the slips of paper, on which each would-be singers would write their name and the number of their song of choice, back to the operator. Kakka wrote down his song without opening the book and handed it back to the lady with a little leer. He then gave me a slip of paper for me to write down my pick.

The list of songs was in Japanese but I wrote down my choice in English. It was *Teenager in Love* by the incomparable Dion and the Belmonts. I assumed they wouldn't be able to read the title but, even if they could, would be unlikely to have the song anyway.

Kakka was grinning widely and glory-bathing in the whole atmosphere of the place where he was the star, surrounded as he by an audience of his employees.

Sailing finished its fading finale and the audience, as all sing-along audiences do, applauded itself wildly.

Kakka made his unsteady but imperious way up the few steps that led to the small, undecorated stage that was raised a couple of feet from the floor. This had two microphones on stands and a spotlight above them threw a dense light straight down, giving the singers deep-sunk eyes, an angry and unhappy droop to their mouths and the appearance of a toothbrush moustache, all of which conjured up the eerie spectre of a certain Austrian dictator.

The already surreal tableau was made even stranger by Kakka grasping the microphone to the unmistakeable strains of Hank

Marvin's intro to Sir Cliff Richard's immortal hit, *Summer Holiday*, and giving it his all. He even tried to emulate the great man's little shuffle and raised lip.

It was absolutely extraordinary and other-worldly. I I was spellbound. I realised, as he sang, that the words were rolling down the screen in Japanese script, phonetically, so the singers just had to make the noises without understanding the lyric at all, no great loss in this case.

I had, by now, worked out that, if you didn't actually know the words, even more humiliation awaited the Westerner in the form of indecipherable Japanese script being your only prompt.

Luckily, I had been word-perfect in my song choice since it was first released when I was nine.

All too soon, Kakka's epic and joyous song came to an end and, as he was taking a bow while making his way off the little stage and down the few steps, I heard the first base twangs and the 'Oooooh, wha ooh whap whap wha ooooh!' of the Belmonts' tight backing harmonies.

I had decided to give it large, emboldened as I was both by being foreign and the bathful of Sake I had imbibed.

My plan was to leap up the stairs, pluck the microphone out of its stand in one electric movement and then turn around to the audience with a boyish, plaintive smile and come straight in with '*Each time we have a quarrel it almost breaks my heart...*' bang on time.

I let Kakka pass me at the bottom of the steps, giving him that private look of respect that passes between us entertainers when we take each other's place in the spotlight, and then leapt onto the stage.

Unfortunately, the ceiling of this construction had been built for performers a lot smaller than me and, as I threw myself upward for maximum dramatic effect, I rammed my head into the ceiling of the raised stage.

For a moment I was stunned and fell to my knees. However, having arrived at the stage in time to strike my planned pose, I was right on time to hit my first line.

The room was lurching before my eyes and being on my knees was probably a good place to be but Doctor Showbiz soon worked his magic and, at the beginning of the second verse I rose, gingerly to my feet, crouching slightly to avoid striking the ceiling again.

Once I realised that there was a little clearance above my head and that only my athletic leap had driven my head into the roofing, there was no stopping me.

Having taken my bow, the crowd bayed for an encore.

I looked at Kakka as I didn't want to steal his thunder, he was my meal-ticket after all, and motioned him to come up on stage for a duet. He shuffled to the steps and gingerly made his way up them.

He was drunker than I had realised and, close up in the unforgiving glare of the spotlight, much older than he had looked in the soft tints of the restaurant. I worried for a moment that he might not make it to the stage. He made this short distance into a lengthy and comic adventure by taking one step up and then retreating down again.

After a few attempts, the spectators set up that sort of audience participation that drunk crowds indulge in all over the world giving a sort of whoop as he mounted a step followed by a disappointed 'ahhhhh' whenever he fell back again.

This became an act in itself and Kakka was happy to indulge his people. But eventually, to tremendous cheers, he arrived onto the stage next to me.

He beamed at me and tried to put his arm around my shoulders but, being considerably shorter than me, his arm could only reach them by his standing on tiptoe, so we performed a rather awkward cuddle to the disconcertion of the crowd who gave a collective, homophobic grunt of disquiet as he nestled his bald head into my armpit.

Kakka motioned to the man running the machine and gave his request in sign language.

There was silence for a while as we waited for the beginning of the song. I had assumed this would be another Cliff belter but was taken aback to hear the unmistakable introductory strains to that twee but classic love song, *Something Stupid*. It was always odd, I felt, that father and daughter Sinatra sang this romantic song to each other, but any misgivings I had about their version paled in comparison to the version I now found myself about to embark on.

Kakka immediately took the initiative as Sinatra père, leaving me to play the part of young Nancy. He entered into the spirit of the number by looking drunkenly into my eyes as he burst into the barely decipherable line, '*I know I stand in line....*'

I smiled weakly back at him, bending my knees to bring myself nearer to his level.

The audience had gone very quiet.

As it came to my turn to sing back to him, I realised I didn't know the words well enough to sing without reference to the song sheet. Kakka had been looking over my shoulder as the words revealed themselves on the screen behind me, so I turned to read them, forgetting that they were written phonetically in Japanese script.

I had a moment of utter, mental confusion before I realised what had happened but turned around and extemporised, making up whatever words I felt were nearest to the original.

Kakka was nothing if not a purist so my manipulation of the words he didn't even understand obviously jarred. But he was a consummate pro and it only phased him for a moment before he was back pouring his heart out in song and gazing into my eyes.

The occasional little noise from the crowd amid the silence, seemed to suggest that the humorous act of young lovers that I thought we were giving was being misrepresented by the crowd and, as I looked at Kakka, I realise that he was, perhaps, also taking the act slightly too literally.

I had no idea what the attitudes were towards homosexuality in Japan then, but I sensed an unnerving and disturbing rustle of homophobia for the second time that night, as Kakka lent nearer and tilted his head towards mine.

With increasing unease, I sang back, solo, the ever more nonsensical words I was making up and then, with more confidence, joining in the chorus.

The song came to an end and, far from the spontaneous explosion of applause we had earnt from our various solo efforts, there was barely a sound.

We turned to the audience and bowed, me with an English courtier's nod and he with a deep, old-fashioned Japanese bow. There was but a smattering of claps. We descended the steps and returned to our seats.

I couldn't help noticing that everyone was wearing a deeply suspicious look and turning their faces away to avoid any eye contact. We had, obviously, committed some sort of cultural solecism.

I wondered if, inventing nonsense for words, I might have inadvertently said something terribly rude or offensive. I turned to Mr Kola who was one of the very few Japanese who had been to the West and London specifically.

'Is everything OK?' I asked nervously. 'Sure,' he answered, 'you both sing good. But....'

'But what?' I turned to face him.

'But, in Japan, two men not sing to each other.' He was obviously being excessively diplomatic.

'Sometimes with each other, like in band' he mimed strumming a guitar. 'But only normal for boy and girl to sing *to* each other, hmmmm.' Here he paused and looked at a point above my head,

'Not very old, important Japanese man and young English man.' He paused and shook his head.

'Not normal at all, no way.' He finished, lapsed into silence and looked at the floor.

No new artiste had taken up the Karaoke cudgel, so silence reigned.

The lights in the gaudy bar seemed even brighter and unforgiving and the noise had returned to that heavy silence that settles in after a very riotous and drunken period, punctuated by a few drunken cries and groans.

'Is he married?' I asked, more for something to say than out of any real interest.

'Mr Kakka? His wife died many years ago. Very sad.' He answered and we both went back to gazing at the floor.

Our reverie was smashed by the first, unmistakeable bars of *Wild Thing*, and an Oriental Trogg leapt onto the stage, gesticulating wildly and grinning diabolically.

This allowed me and Mr Kola to look up and smile again.

I leant towards him and, in the hiatus before the opening words '*Wild Thing, I think I love you...*', I said loudly, 'I'm married.'

'Aha,' said Kola 'that's good.'

'Yes,' I continued, waiting for the next quiet bit, 'but my wife is not dead.'

'Also good.' he replied. 'Living wife best sort.'

'That depends.' I joked, as I rather thought we might have got a bit of East-West banter going.

He looked at me, horrified, and said, quite loudly,

'No! Living wife always best. Dead wife no good.' He gave me an appalled look.

I wondered just what his idea of the stereotypical Englishman was and whether I had confirmed or shattered it.

Certainly, Mr Kola was not the cruel, impersonal character I'd had entrenched in my mind.

'I was just joking.' I said, smiling broadly, hoping that perhaps I had appealed to what I believed to be his countrymen's love of mean humour.

This seemed to make things worse, and I realised that our stereotypes had been reversed. He was looking at me with his mouth pursed, shaking his head slowly.

I had lost respect. I was a heartless cynic and perhaps even a seducer of old widowers.

Mr Kakka had quietly nodded off and Mr Kola said. 'We take Kakka Sama home now.'

'Should I come with you? I asked, I was now a bit at sea with the etiquette and keen not to make any more blunders.

'Of course, you are our guest.' He said and he started to organise a lifting party for Mr Kakka.

Three young men in suits lifted the unconscious old man and carried him towards the door. I followed in their wake as everyone leapt out of the way, pulling any slumped figures of comatose drunks out of the way like so much flotsam before a royal barge.

Outside he was bundled into the back of his limo while I was motioned into the front. I assumed that I was being put out of temptation's way so I wouldn't be sitting next to the lifeless old codger.

Nobody had seemed the slightest surprised by his performance or worried by his having to be carried out or, indeed, by the host of other men who had surrendered first to Bacchus and then Morpheus.

I was to learn that any behaviour, short of real violence or humiliation, was tolerated and forgotten the next morning when the slate was rubbed clean and the men who worked for this company returned to the minutely stratified world from which they had escaped for a short while.

It was an interesting concept that worked well in a naturally well- ordered, obedient and deferential society but would break down on its first night's trial in Britain when any passing squaddies would immediately take advantage of a prone old codger for urinary target practice.

I was delivered back to my hotel and then up to my room by Mr Kola to find a man asleep on a sort of bench outside. Kola woke this gentleman and introduced him to me, explaining that he was there to get me anything I might need in the night and to deliver me safely to their headquarters by 7:30 the next morning.

For my next few visits to Tokyo, while under the aegis of this company, these were the conditions of their regime.

When I arrived at their offices the next morning, feeling indescribable and having had only a very few hours' sleep, Mr Kakka was already there, beaming and neat as a pin.

Nothing was mentioned about the previous night, and I remained silent. Some of the human detritus from the karaoke bar were also shining and smiling happily and there was nothing to suggest any overindulgence the night before.

It was a phenomenon I was to encounter again and again after long nights of drinking, singing and generally laddish behaviour by every stratum of the company and, although I became used to the communal amnesia, to begin with it was rather like being in an episode of *The Twilight Zone*.

I was relieved to find that Mr Kakka was not in love with me, and that Mr Kola again treated me with his initial respect and courtesy, but I could detect an underlying sense of distaste.

This would only increase through the years we 'worked together' as he saw how clay-like Western feet really were, how sandy our foundations and how impervious to the grace of their culture most of us were.

2

I Had A Grate Fall

Many years ago, a friend of mine decided to have a Guy Fawkes party before work began at a dilapidated house that was about to be renovated. It was to start with fireworks in the garden and then carry on inside. The house could take some battering as it was being gutted anyway but, as the electricity and water were turned off, it promised to be a somewhat chaotic affair.

When we arrived, the enormous amounts of drink already supplied by our host had been swollen by the bounty the guests had brought.

On top of the mighty firework display he had organised himself, some guests had brought their own arsenal of smaller, more dangerous and easier to misuse bangers, squibs and even a few military-strength thunder-flashes which exploded with a window rattling, ear-splitting noise having been designed to replicate the sound and fury of a genuine battlefield.

This was an incendiary mixture in every sense and, without the need to protect the house or garden, the dangerous pyrotechnics in the hands of some very irresponsible people were being used in ways not recommended on the box or by the M.o.D.

Anarchy was in the air and also, perhaps, the smell of weed hinting at the sort of mutinous undercurrent that would have made an experienced crowd-control policeman call for extensive back-up.

It was difficult not to feel a bit carried away by this mood. The atmosphere felt as I imagined it did amongst the *sans-culottes* in revolutionary Paris. There was a palpable sizzle of insurrection among these rebels-without-any-cause-at-all in North London that evening, a mere two centuries on from their French counterparts.

Some heroic amounts of alcohol had been drunk and everyone was full of barbecued meat and potatoes so, by the time the firework display was ready to launch, there was a very unstable crowd of human blue touchpaper milling about.

The fireworks began, as they always do, with much ooh-ing and ahh-ing, but those armed with their own ammunition began to join in, so things suddenly became very precarious. A few people tried to calm things but the insurgents' blood was up and the wheels were coming off the tumbrils.

The noise and flash of explosions both above our heads and at ground level were like a creeping barrage on the Somme. In the midst of this bedlam I heard someone scream out a pantomime warning,

'Theo, behind you, watch out.'

I ducked assuming a missile was coming my way. Nothing arrived but the shouts continued so I spun around again. There still appeared to be nothing coming towards me so I assumed it was just good-natured but low-level pranking. Still the warnings continued, and I whirled around like a foolish dog chasing its tail but there was still nothing.

'Jesus, Theo, behind you!'

This last call had a note of desperate urgency but too late I heard the sinister hissing very close indeed behind me and smelt the unmistakable whiff of cordite.

With a noise like the first, close crack of thunder, a large banger exploded in the back pocket of my jeans. I suppose a veteran of some hideous battle, taken unawares by a grenade, might have known how to react but, in the melee of fireworks dropping all around me, I was completely stunned and bewildered.

Moments later a keen, stinging pain began in my left buttock followed by a dull throb and then the cold, chill wind hit my naked flesh. The firework had blown off the pocket of my jeans as well as the under-patch of denim and made a sizeable hole in my underpants. It had also taken a very unsightly divot out of my arse so my burnt and blistered buttock was now open to the elements.

From the looks on the faces of the first to arrive on the scene and examine it, the wound was obviously not a pretty sight but, of course, I couldn't see it.

As always after an accident, there were some unconvincing medical theories put forward by self-professed experts as to how best to treat this kind of wound but, when no consensus was reached, everyone got bored and wandered away telling me it would 'probably be best just to leave it to mend in its own time'.

As there was such a lack of sympathy, I limped off to get a drink.

Nobody had owned up or apologised for this assault, but I harboured grave suspicions of one 'friend'.

I watched the rest of the incendiary and unnerving display in quite some pain, but a glass of whiskey thrown onto my injury by someone who professed to be an expert on battlefield wounds and a few others thrown down my throat made it bearable and the throbbing soon subsided, as did the fireworks.

It was cold, now, as the bonfire had all but spluttered out so I made my painful way back to the house. It had no electricity and, as there were only a few candles, making out anything at all was difficult.

A portable tape machine, wired up to a couple of speakers, blared out loud, tinny music.

Through the French windows I could make out people moving in a large, empty room. I stumbled into the semi-darkness and, while my eyes were adjusting, a voice I recognised said,

'Come on, let's have a dance.'

It was my friend Laura.

She dragged me into the centre of the heaving mass of shadowy figures. I put my drink down and stuffed my hands deep into the pockets of my jeans in the careless, nonchalant way I affected in those days to look cool. We shifted, in the way you do when dancing, from here to there, bumping into people and bouncing off them like soft, human dodgems.

After shuffling about for a while, we found ourselves by a chimneypiece above which was a large, lone mirror in which I could enjoy watching my Elvis moves. I was just wondering why a single wall hanging had been left in the house when I suddenly found myself pitched violently forward over what turned out to be a club fender and hurtling, head-first, into the stygian void. Unable to get my hands out of my pockets, I had nothing to save myself with and so dived with force into the wrought-iron grate.

I sensed the dark shape of the ironwork rushing towards me at speed and, when I hit it, there was absolutely no give at all. The highest of the iron struts struck my top lip and front teeth like a hammer but there was little noise, except that of my rolling over into the fireplace after the initial collision.

My two front teeth shattered straight away and my top lip burst like a plum. I was face down and bent awkwardly backwards with my legs still in the air over the fender. A few kind people helped me up, awkwardly and ignobly, and I was finally able to pull my hands out of my pockets and feel my mouth and teeth.

They were unrecognisable to my fingers or my tongue and burned with jagged pain with every breath of the frigid air.

Laura, having recovered from a bout of hysterical laughter, fired up a lighter to have a proper look and grimaced at what she saw. I could see the damage, illuminated by the flame and reflected in the mirror, and I could see her point.

The wounds were made to look even worse by the soot plastered down one side of my face and there were matted hair and smears of blood over my cheeks and chin. The whole picture was given an even more Gothic look by the flickering flame beneath my head which threw a vast shadow onto the wall.

Someone had told my wife, Louise, that I might have had an accident - or even two, as she was still unaware of the banger fiasco - so she had come to find me. In the sinister half-light, my face, and indeed my bottom, must have presented a repulsive sight and the wounds must have looked severe.

So much so that Louise was moved to say,

'Ouch, that looks painful.' And then wander away. muttering 'idiot'.

There was no running water and finding something to bathe and clean my face was difficult. Both the fizzy and still water had run out, so I cleansed my wounds with a bottle of ginger ale. This stung badly but reassured me that it was doing some good and I patted off the remaining blood and teased the wounded flesh down with a handkerchief doused in vodka. An hour later the party was beginning to break up and my entire body was aching, stinging and throbbing in roughly that order.

We had been warned that the police were taking an interest in anyone leaving the party and so might be waiting to ambush any unwary and inebriated drivers.

Louise had sensibly left, I certainly didn't make a particularly appetising passenger but, eventually, an old friend who had not been drinking offered me a ride home.

This friend had been deaf since his late teens when he had contracted meningitis. He lived a very full and fun-filled life with amazing tenacity and lip-read incredibly well. He spoke though, like many deaf people who could once hear, with an unusual pattern of speech and timbre that led some people, who were not used to it, to think he might be drunk even when he wasn't.

In normal times you would try to avoid letting him drive as, between watching your lips rather than the road and his natural proclivity for speed, his driving could result in genuinely bottom-clenching trips.

But needs must and in great pain, with a throbbing head, still quite drunk and wracked by deep misgivings, I climbed into his passenger seat. As always, he had left the inside light on, the better to lipread and, as he shot off, I tried to explain about keeping an eye out for the police.

My lips, in their ruptured state, were not easy to read so we made our way onto the main suburban road without him really having understood my warnings about the possibility of a police presence.

Travelling at great speed with the car lit from within, made it difficult to seet what was happening outside the car but, through the blur, I saw a hint of blue lights.

I tried to draw his attention to this but, having turned towards me when I hit his arm, he saw the policeman with his hand held up to stop us and braked just in time to bring us to a halt very close to him.

'Whadda's going on?' My friend asked in his unique voice.

My mouth was, by now, barely moving and my lips felt like two pillows.

'I dolt you..the hlease were aiting.' I said as best I could,

'Whadda?' He asked.

'The hlease!' I pointed to the side window where a policeman's head had appeared as he knocked against it, trying to attract my friend's attention.

'Who's dat? He asked following my eyes.

'It's the hucking hleace!' I repeated. 'Turn the light ovv.'

'Wadda they want?' He asked. 'I haven't done anyting wrong, I haven't had anyting to drink.'

'Ell good,' I was sounding like a very bad ventriloquist, 'just do hot he says.'

'Whadda?' He repeated. I opened my window as another policeman had arrived at my side.

'Bloody hell,' He said, recoiling, 'what happened to you?'

'Long story, oshicer.' I tried to look sober and wretched but philosophical. 'I hell into the hirelace.' I explained.

'You what?' He asked.

I was tiring of this banter and the other policeman was having his own problems with my friend who had been asked to step out of the car and into the dark where a series of verbal misunderstandings was being enacted,

'Go into the light,' I said to his policeman. 'so he can read your lisss, your lisss', and with a flash of pain I made myself purse my lips. 'Read your lips.'

'Why?' Said Sherlock.

'Because he's hucking death, death.....deaf.' I finally managed.

'Oh, right, why didn't you say so?' He asked

'Uuuuuh, I did.' I said

'And so what's wrong with you then?' He asked.

I had also walked into the lights and he now saw my battered face.

I turned around to motion the other policeman into the light hoping he might explain my plight as my mouth was seizing up and speech was becoming even more painful, but he merely added.

'What happened to your behind, if I might ask, Sir?'

I mimed a banger being lit and put into my back pocket and then opening hands and arms in the universal sign language for an explosion.

Both policemen winced.

'On purpose, Sir? Someone did that on purpose?' The first rozzer asked. 'They need teaching a lesson. If they only knew what we have to deal with on Fireworks Night they wouldn't behave like stupid kids.'

He was wrong but I nodded sagely and shrugged and then said, ' I hink it was an accident.'

'And what happened to your face, Sir?' He asked.

'Ell, as I hos telling your hend here, I was dancing wi' a girl and I hell into the hire lace.'

'What, Sir?'

'The hire lace....where you ha a hire hen it gets cold.' I explained with more charades.

'Wadda you saying?' Said my friend.

'But I'm hine now. Can ee go home, leeeeez?' I begged.

'You,' the first policeman said, turning around to my friend 'have you been drinking, Sir?'

'Waddid he say?' He asked me.

'He ants to know if you have been drinking!' I mouthed as overtly as I could and mimed liquid being poured down a throat.

'No, nothing, zero.' He said, making an O with his thumb and forefinger and turning back to the policeman who was bending into his car to get something out so his next words were lost on my friend.

'He's pissed as a rat.' I heard him say to his colleague.

'No, no he's not.' I said, bending to talk to the policeman. 'I'm hissed as a rat ut he's just desh!'

'Whadda you saying?' Asked my friend.

'I'm telling them that you're not hissed just desh?' I said.

'Wadda?' He said

'Oh, I see Sir, deaf.' Said the second policeman.

'Why didn't you just say so?'

'I've een trying to.' I said.

'Wadda?' Said my friend.

We got back into the car.

I had a terrible thirst and I was as cold as I have ever been. I suspected that I might die of any number of things before I got home and so his driving no longer held any terror for me.

Nonetheless, when he switched on the light at ninety miles an hour and turned his face around in front of mine to ask,

'Whadda was all thad about?' A slither of apprehension ran through me.

3

HELLISH ANGELS

As anyone who has ever driven with me will attest, I am not at one with mechanical things.

When, in my later teens, I spent the holidays in the middle of the Yorkshire dales, I needed something to get around on. This was mainly to travel to cricket, golf, the pub or even the throbbing metropolis of York for entertainment.

I was, to begin with, underage for a driving licence so, as many did, I got around this by using a moped which you were allowed to drive, if you sported a learner's plate, from the age of sixteen. The machine had to be under 50cc so the most popular choice was a Honda 50.

When I first got mine, it had satchels at either side, a large mudguard and a footwell contraption that made it look what it was, something for old ladies and postmen to potter about on. Along with these trimmings its riders invariably wore a pudding-bowl leather crash helmet with a peak and old flying goggles.

This was not a very sexy look, so I knew I would be ridiculed almost anywhere but certainly on arrival at butch sporting contests.

As I never passed my driving test, I drove this little beauty for nearly three years.

I stripped this Honda down to its absolute basics with the result that it looked like a French velo rather than the dirt track bike

I had hoped for and, if it rained or I had to drive through mud, which was often, I would be liberally covered in grime.

However, I could tell people at school that, in the holidays, I got around on a Honda motorbike. I just avoided conversations with any real motorbike enthusiasts and deflected any questions about its cc size or anything else that might give me away.

It sometimes surprised the very occasional date I might get in the middle of the Yorkshire dales that I turned up on this skeletal thing rather than a car or, at least a proper motorbike. It was only bearable for a pillion in the summer, and it was a keen girl indeed who would agree to go on the back of my Honda 50 in the rain.

I never met one of these girls.

A boy at my school, sophisticated beyond his years and who knew everything about girls, had told me that, if you rode over bumpy roads for more than ten minutes with a lady riding pillion, she would become so overcome with lust that, the moment you stopped the bike, she would drag you into the nearest field or building site in order to sate this ardour.

I never met one of these girls either.

Still, the Honda 50 gave me a sort of gossamer-thin attachment to the 'brotherhood of bikers' and I may well have exaggerated to some people both the size of my machine and the extent of my riding skills.

Thus it was that a relation of mine asked me if a friend of his could leave his bike, apparently his pride and joy, with me in Yorkshire while he drove up to Scotland. I agreed.

A very smooth-looking young man, probably only five years older than me but decades older in cool-years, turned up on this unbelievably powerful, exotic and terrifying looking thing.

It was beautiful and shiny, a work of art on wheels, and I could instantly see why people might become obsessed with such things.

I introduced myself and showed him where he should store the brute.

'Thanks so much for doing this.' He said as we walked over to the house to wait for his lift. I say he walked but, in reality, he moseyed.

As we passed my Honda he said,

'Where do you keep yours?'

'My what?'

'Your hog?' he said laconically.

I was baffled for a moment, we were, after all, in a very rustic setting. 'Your bike?' he continued, 'Guy tells me you're a biker.'

'Oh yes, yes, my hog. Ah, actually it's being repaired at the moment.'

'Have a prang?' he asked, and I realised my small lie was quickly becoming awkward but there was still time to get it back on track but I took the wrong route.

'Yeah, 'fraid so, quite nasty, actually.'

'Bad luck.' He said. 'You OK?' he asked thoughtfully.

'Oh yeah,' I said. 'been in worse, you know.' My mind turned to my rather nasty brush with a hedgerow in Stillington and then falling off when a sapling sprang back and soaked my cricket whites.

'Certainly do.' He said and rolled up the leg of his jeans to show me a scar that a survivor of D-Day would have been proud of.

'Occupational hazard for us.' He continued breezily and slapped me on the back.

'I thought that might be it.' He said throwing out a hand.

'Be what?'

'Your bike.' He said and I could see he was pointing at the Honda 50.

'What?' I roared with laughter, 'God no, Christ no...that? God no.'

'Only joking.' he said.

His lift arrived and we walked out to the car and I bent down to say hello to the driver through the window.

'Be careful with his bike and do not have a go on it.' He said to me grinning. 'It's the thing he loves most in the world and probably the only Electra Glide in Yorkshire.'

They were setting off when the biker lowered his window and said, 'What's yours, then?'

'My what?'

'Your bike....the one that's being mended?'

'Ah, a Honda.' I said.

'Nice bikes.' He said nodding his head. 'Which one?'

'Japanese.' I replied.

'No, which one...what cc?'

'Oh right,' I said. '500.'

I told myself I had only added a nought.

'CP? Twin?' He asked.

'Yep, um, yep.' I mumbled and laughed and waved as they drove off crunching through the potholes in the drive.

I was left alone, standing by my absurd little Honda 50, wondering again why I had told an untruth that gave me no personal advantage to someone I might never see again.

Pride and self-aggrandisement, I concluded.

I snapped myself out of this moment of self-chastisement and wandered over to the shed where the chrome-plated animal was propped up, quivering in the shards of light that were raking it through the slits in the roof, looking as if it might just take off, riderless, into an indie film.

I looked it over and then sat on its huge seat, scrunched up my eyes and made loud engine noises, squatting forward into an imaginary wind.

I had recently seen *Easy Rider*.

The next morning was perfectly beautiful, and I found myself alone in the house. I dressed and looked out of the window across the Dales towards the A1, the old Roman road to York, as straight as an arrow, a biker's dream.

I wondered whether I dared take the beast out for a spin.

My doubts had nothing to do with the legality of doing this nor the chances of crashing and harming someone else's property. It was just pure lack of nerve and confidence in driving something so terrifying.

I wandered over to the hut and squinted at the brute again.

It really was very big, considerably larger than the stripped-down motorbikes you mostly saw in those days. Apart from anything else, I just couldn't see how you could prop it up when it was stationary.

I sat on it again and then got off and moved it forward off its rest and it immediately began to pull me over with its enormous weight and I started to do a little shuffle-footed dance, making squeaking noises, trying to stop it from falling over and only just managed to pull it back upright before it crushed my calf.

This dented my confidence.

I didn't like to think what damage I might do to the bike just by letting it fall over without even riding it.

With some difficulty I managed to push it out of the barn and onto the drive and wheeled the brute onto a flat piece of gravel. I had at least started a big bike before but my antipathy towards any sort of machinery meant that it wasn't by any means plain sailing, and I struggled to get any response from the machine.

Now astride and, at first, decidedly uncomfortable, I finally got a throaty roar out of it. I had already hit my ankle twice on what I thought was the starter before I realized it had nothing to do with anything.

God knows why, I very gently opened the throttle and the bike moved forward and the stand pinged back. There was absolutely no way I could keep it upright while moving so slowly so I opened it up a little more and, even at this pedestrian speed it began to frighten me. I could barely stay astride so I decided to accelerate down the drive and onto the proper road.

Once on the tarmac, things seemed to go a bit smoother though I was still loath to go at a speed that would, counterintuitively, have made handling this lump of metal much easier.

I was by no means in the clear as negotiating the narrow, winding, hedgerow lined lanes meant only a minimum speed was possible and I was already exhausted by the effort.

I could hear nothing above the angry roar of the bike or see very much and I rounded every bend expecting to meet the same fate as Lawrence of Arabia.

Though mine would be slower and not written about.

I began to have profound respect for anyone who drove a large bike and the Isle of Man TT races suddenly made no sense at all.

It was while battling with this collection of random thoughts that I came to a junction and just missed a car by inches that must have assumed it had the right of way.

My immediate feelings were mixed.

There was terror, of course, and relief at having evaded the Grim Reaper, but also a sense of elation when I looked back to see the driver shaking his fist at me.

Bloody biker, bloody typical, he was probably shouting and for me to be included, even for that moment, amongst that anarchic brotherhood gave me a real, even if unearned, thrill.

This incident had also given me a bit more confidence and soon I came to a wider road leading to the A1. I leaned slightly into the left turn, much easier it transpired for some reason than the right turn, and, without looking to see if anything was coming, I continued onto the road.

Up ahead was a pub.

My lack of confidence and experience in how to stop and balance the brute on one foot had made me a slave to perpetual motion and a car shot past, swerving to avoid me, but I didn't feel the same thrill as I had earlier, in fact it gave me a gut-wrenching shock.

I came onto the pub courtyard and slowed to a merciful stop. I struggled to keep the bike upright and to prop it up but, after some embarrassing pulling to and fro I had it standing and still.

The silence was deafening.

I went into the pub, in fact I ambled into the pub like a gunslinger into a saloon and ordered a pint of cider. Probably not, I admit, Billy the Kid's usual tipple but I was very thirsty.

I certainly hadn't gone over 60 mph but that had been quite fast enough and, it turned out, too fast to smoke while riding.

I took my pint out to the back of the pub and sat down to enjoy it with a cigarette and a manly feeling of the world, or at least that part of Yorkshire, being my oyster.

I finished my drink and walked back to the front of the pub and had just sat astride the bike when a mighty roaring noise heralded the arrival of a fleet of motorbikes coming into the courtyard.

I didn't want to get involved with them at all so I was trying to start the bike when a few of them, dismounted with practised ease, and wandered over towards me.

The first to arrive wore his *Easy Rider* garb with such a natural confidence that I became aware of my own clothes and was just wondering if jeans, plimsolls, Aertex shirt and a cricket jersey was thought cool anywhere when he suddenly stood still and said,

'Fuck me,'

His colleagues had caught him up and now stood around him also staring at the bike.

'Fuck me.' Was the most popular response as they gazed in wonder at the Harley-Davidson. Their collective accents seemed to be Geordie though there was a definite Brummie twang to one of the 'fooks'.

'Fuck me, an Electra Glide.' Said the original man who seemed to be the leader of whatever they were.

'Yours?' He asked pointing.

'Yeapp.' I said in a vaguely American accent.

'You a Yank?' He asked and I replied,

'No, from just up the road.' And added, stupidly, 'Actually.'

For a moment they were thrown by my lack of obvious provenance.

'Fucking Electra Glide, unbe-fucking-lieavable.' He said and they gathered round me asking questions about the machine that I could only answer with an enigmatic look and a shrug.

'Go on,' one said 'let's see what she can do.'

'Gotta get home.' I said with modestly raised eyebrows and a sort of cavalier grin as if someone was waiting for me to rescue them. My new accent was getting nearer to John Wayne's than I'd hoped.

'Come on, mate, just a bit down the road.'

Up close, they were an eclectic crew but the mixture of rather wan train-spotter types and sad mechanics had enough ugly and threatening looking people, complete with rude tattoos and scars, for me not to want to disappoint them.

To my delight, the engine started and I made my way slowly down the incline to the road.

There was a scramble behind me as they rushed back to get on their bikes. For the moment I was alone and looking for a place to turn around and go home.

Being on a wider road made a huge difference as now I could tool along at what appeared to be vast speed but which, when I consulted the speedometer, turned out to be 40 mph and I could now see miles ahead and had plenty of room to manoeuvre.

I don't like sharing danger with a contraption.

I have realised that I am, if anything, a solo risk-taker or at least of those taken with other humans and prefer to be unencumbered by metal or machinery.

I had decided to go around the first roundabout and return the way I had come and go home, park the bike, and revel in the sense of achievement and I was moving along nicely, even beginning to enjoy the ride. There was no sign of the pub bikers when I caught sight of something in my peripheral vision.

I looked over my shoulder to find a small gaggle of motorbikes behind me and others coming up beside me.

As the first member shot past me, waving and pointing at my bike, thumbs up and grinning, I noticed, for the first time, the Hell's Angels insignia on the back of his leather waistcoat.

Good Lord, I was among a chapter.

I remember thinking how risible it was that a chapter of this much-feared organisation should manifest itself in the rustic setting of the Yorkshire Dales and that perhaps they were only in fancy dress.

But, as more of them drew level, pointing at my bike, I realised they were obviously as amazed to see such a hog in motion in these surroundings as I was in seeing them.

I was now all but surrounded by this horde who were a mixed bag of single riders and others with their dates on pillions, of all ages and with a strange spectrum of evil-looking bikes.

These had every possible variation of handlebar, seat and decoration to make each seem uniquely primitive and offensive. But what the riders all had in common was that, on their bikes, they all suddenly looked like Hell's Angels, an impossible thing to recreate unless you are prepared to put the grimy hours and refuse to indulge in any bodily or oral hygiene for many years.

I was now trapped in the middle of their chapter and, as they accelerated around me, I had no choice but to go faster and faster.

Luckily the noise of the bikes drowned out my snivelling, terrified squeals and I hoped that my tears would be mistaken for ones forced from my eyes by the speed we were going, which was now much too fast.

As some of them came ridiculously close, better to see my bike, I tried desperately not to shy away to avoid hitting the bikes sandwiching me on the other side travelling a hairsbreadth away.

To my horror I saw a sign for the A1, a triumph of Roman roadbuilding and long famous as the place boy-racers and their ilk went to 'open up' their machines.

Some of them took turns in nipping to my side, studying the engine up very close, and then darting away like swallows.

I was, as far as my speed and direction was concerned, at their mercy but they seemed to be treating me with some respect. This was, I can only suspect because of the bike itself and, as I hadn't expected anything other than a potter, the fact I was wearing no helmet. The latter was not compulsory in those days though most people did wear one, but the more raffish element tended to go bareheaded.

Surrounded, I was forced further down the A1.

As we bombed along this aerodrome of a surface, they started to accelerate to 60 and then 70 mph.

I realised they were preparing for a 'ton up' a slang expression in those days for doing 100 mph on a public highway.

Speed limits had only recently been introduced on motorways so what they were considering brought two of my deepest fears into play, death and prison.

I really didn't want to do this at all and started to jerk my thumb back over my shoulder to signify that I had to go back from whence I had come, possibly to save someone from a fearsome fate. This action was unbelievably frightening as it meant driving with one hand as I gesticulated with the other.

I was in a terrible funk, both physically and mentally and, while I was beginning to feel ever more out of control in every sense, I saw a roundabout coming up.

Sweet Jesus, I thought, realising that, at this speed, there was no hope of completing the manoeuvre I needed to execute in order to point myself homeward.

We came to this obstacle at an absurd speed, no thought had been given by these tearaways that there might be other cars on this roundabout or who had the right of way as we crossed it. Suddenly, with a little dip to their left then right, followed by an immediate righting of their bikes, they negotiated the obstacle.

I, on the other hand, was forced by lack of technique to take a much straighter course, missing both the curb surrounding the roundabout and then the curb surrounding the continuing road by mere inches.

I now had no choice but to carry on to the next roundabout and somehow navigate my way around it and to go back home.

Mercifully one appeared quite soon or I would have soon found myself in the Home Counties.

I tried to message them with nods of my head that I was going back which they seemed to understand as they began to wave.

I tried to decrease my speed but, as we hit the roundabout I was still going much too fast and, nervously decelerating into it forced the bike right. This caused the back wheel to execute a series of wobbling slaloms and the best I could manage was to force the bike into the first right turning where a small queue of cars watched me brake very hard, swerve to the right of the road and gently fall sideways, withdrawing my leg just in time to avoid any serious damage.

I had survived.

The bike continued to make a revving noise for a while but I turned it off and sat down on its side, exhausted.

It took me a few seconds to realise that the engine was burning my thigh badly but I was too drained to make any noise or indeed care, so I just rolled off and onto the grass.

I studied the sky, not without some pleasure and pride, I had ridden with the Angels, on my first time out.

Unbelievable really, I thought, and allowed myself a wry smile.

That was the upside.

The bike was lying on its downside like a metal beetle needing to be righted and I noticed some distinct scratches and marks that hadn't been there before. They also looked as if no amount of polishing would fix them.

I had no idea where these had come from.

When my brief moment of relief and euphoria had melted away, I took more realistic stock.

I was now a very long way from home and the day was not as balmy as it had been and I calculated that, if I travelled at the speed at which I felt safe, it would take me a few hours to get home.

I stood the bike up with much effort accompanied by catcalls from passing motorists and started it quite easily, having feared it might never work again.

Relieved, I pondered the day, or at least the short time it had taken me to travel unintentionally down England's spine and many other things besides.

I would have to get the bike done up and replace the petrol.

I would never do this again.

I was unharmed apart from a grazed knuckle that I hadn't noticed and the burnt thigh.

I wanted to go home and watch telly.

I pushed the bike for a short distance but it seemed to fight me all the way. It was much too heavy to get far and I realised I would be lucky to get home at all so there was nothing for it but to get back in the saddle.

I made my way back onto the A1 and rode very slowly indeed back the way I had come, still shaking and occasionally shouting out involuntarily each time I remembered a salty part of the ride. I think this is called flashback.

At last, as dusk settled, I was in sight of home.

I had gained no more confidence on the bike than I'd had earlier and had absolutely no desire to ride one ever again but, as I wended my weary way back up the drive, I mused, with some satisfaction, that I had achieved an ambition that I had never actually held nor one that would ever have occurred to me, I had ridden in a Ton Up with The Hell's Angels.

I felt rather dauntless.

4

CRASH COURSES

Of the many motoring mishaps that have befallen me, the one that stands out in stark relief, does so because I was utterly to blame and it led to the owner of the car developing an unshakeably low opinion of me until the day she died.

I have hopes that the retelling may prove cathartic and allow me that modern invention, closure.

These hopes are low.

I was staying with my friend Ali and his adorable parents at their place in the country. His wonderful and kind father always seemed to be amused by me and we had very funny chats which often reduced both of us to tears of laughter. Nonetheless, he rightly took me for a 'chaotic character' in his words and probably not a sound influence on his son.

His mother was another matter. She was extremely elegant and brave and could easily have taken on a crowd of football hooligans single handed. She'd had a tough earlier life yet weathered every storm with great dignity, kindness and selflessness.

However, she was not amused by me at all.

Although they were a well-off family, she would squeeze every piece of almost finished soap together with others to make one new, marbleised bar in a strange machine that I had never seen before. Every sauce bottle stood upside down in her cupboards to save the last drop and anything left on a plate or in a cup was recycled. The half empty glasses of whiskey I often abandoned, dotted about the house, would be arraigned accusingly by my place at the breakfast table.

She was absolutely convinced that I had been sent by dark forces to drag her son down into moral oblivion.

Her household thrift was an affectionate running joke and she and I often battled over my leaving the electric fire on in my room, as the heating was always off and the house was freezing. However, all of us saw it as a rather charming eccentricity for she was, above all, a very kind and decent woman.

She adored Louise and, after we married, always hugged her closely on seeing her, like a mother might a daughter who had just escaped from Jack the Ripper. I was tolerated mainly for Louise's sake. That is not to say I wasn't very fond of Ali's mother, I was, but I realised that, even though she always treated me with great politeness, I was anathema to her and only by working for no reward in a refugee camp somewhere very dangerous for many years, could I possibly have wheedled my way back into her esteem.

One Saturday morning, I had arranged a game of golf. Ali had naively left his car for me to use, but warned me that, if it didn't start, as was often the case, his mother's new car was arriving that morning and as a very last resort she might give me a lift.

I woke later than I should have, hungover and confused. Remembering I was meant to be at the golf course, I dragged on some clothes, found my clubs and ran down to Ali's car but, try as I might, it wouldn't start. With no mobiles it was impossible to contact the other players and I started to panic. There is little I hate more than keeping people waiting for anything, especially games, so I went upstairs and asked Louise to help push the car.

She got up, not too happily, and pushed the wretched machine until she was exhausted by the fruitless exertion. You might ask why I didn't push and I can think of no truthful answer that might show me in a better light. It still wouldn't start, mainly because I had no idea how to jump-start a car and Louise rightly refused to push any more.

Parked on the drive near Ali's car, I noticed his mother's gleaming, new red motor with its keys in so I went into the house to try and find Ali's mother, but she had disappeared.

Then I made a really appalling decision.

Instead of calling the golf club, explaining my predicament and asking them to tell my friends I wouldn't be turning up, I decided to take matters into my own hands and grasp the nettle, or in this case, the keys to the new car. Louise was unconvinced by this plan and tried her very best to stop me, I could see her wondering, not for the first time, just what kind of marriage she had got herself into. But I insisted Ali had said it would be fine and asked her to come with me to map-read and, with huge reluctance, she agreed only, I believe, to keep an eye on me.

I was never a fast driver nor a boy racer, I was just inept. Trying to find the golf course going as fast as I dared in third gear while sweating out last night's whiskey did not present me at my most lovable and, by the time we reached the golf course, Louise was planning her future life as a happy divorcee.

It turned out to have all been to no avail as I was too late and the others had started twenty minutes earlier without me.

I was tetchy.

'Right, well, we'll just have to go back. Look out for a tobacconist, I need some fags and some Lucozade...and something to eat.' I seem to remember that I may have said this in a way that intimated Louise was somehow to blame for the situation.

In turn, she was quite obviously and rightly both furious with me and disappointed by my performance while I was only really upset to have missed the golf.

We set off at a sedate pace, I had resolved to go very carefully and behave graciously on the drive back so as to try and undo some of the damage caused by my petulance but I wasn't being as gracious as I might have been. Urging Louise to look out for somewhere that sold cigarettes clearly irritated her further.

We were no more than tooling along the country roads while desperately looking for a tobacconist, which any desperate smoker knows is like searching for a unicorn when you're out of fags.

Louise was reading the map.

'You turn left here...HERE.' She said when, just on the other side of a little village road, I saw the very shop I needed.

'There. There.' I cried out, pointing.

I swung the car left but, I wasn't looking left as I was squinting at the cigarette shop to see if it was open.

Suddenly, there was a terrible grinding, metallic noise, the car stopped dead and both of us were thrown forward. I had no idea what had happened.

Then there was a serpentine hissing and a mist somehow appeared. It evaporated to reveal that we were pointing upwards, suspended by some unseen force, behind a truck.

I had failed to see a lorry, parked on the corner and I had driven into the iron girder sticking out of its back. It had pierced the bonnet and lifted us up into the air.

As I watched the front of the car crumple before my eyes I may have screamed.

Louise said. 'You've just driven into an iron girder.'

'What? Where?' I answered, these were both good questions.

'You've driven into a lorry with an iron girder sticking out of it and it's gone through the bonnet and into the engine.' She sounded pleased for the first time that day.

At this moment, with a terrible, metallic shriek, the truck just drove off.

The girder unsheathed itself from the bonnet, causing a truly hellish noise as the car bounced back down onto the road. The truck calmly disappeared up the road, its driver blissfully unaware of the misery that would unfold after his departure.

I got out of the car to take stock.

There was a huge hole in the bonnet like a bayonet wound and there was a hissing noise from the engine.

I was worried there might even be bits of the engine missing but, as I didn't know what a complete engine looked like, I couldn't tell. The new car couldn't have looked worse but I pointed out to a disturbingly quiet but unhurt Louise that most of the damage was probably superficial.

I sat back while the full enormity of what I had done swept over me and repeated. 'Oh my God, oh sweet Jesus.' Again, and again.

I looked around to Louise for sympathy, but I recognised the hint of a smirk and possibly even a touch of *schadenfreude* in her demeanour.

But, on the bright side, no one was injured and we were near a village shop so I went in to buy all my necessary supplies.

'Did you see that?' I asked the man behind the counter.

'The crash, the truck?' He replied.

'Yes,' I said, 'it could have been very serious.' I paid for my odd selection of things.

'Yes.' He shrugged his shoulders and shook his head slowly and added,

'Arsehole.'

'I know, really dangerous stopping a truck there like that.' I answered.

'No, mate, he said, 'I mean you. It had a fucking great flag on it.'

It wasn't the time to lecture him on the traditional salesman-customer relationship.

I was in a horrible, bowel-constricted state when I got back into the car. Louise was still scarily quiet. I ate a Mars bar, drank half a large bottle of Lucozade and lit up a cigarette.

What to do?

I started the engine and it seemed to work despite the horrific-looking damage. As we tooled along very slowly, I pondered the state of play. How Ali's mother was going to react was impossible to imagine but, to the positive, my stock was so low with her that it couldn't get any worse. This was good.

On the other hand, Ali would be furious, his father deeply disappointed and Louise might well leave me, this was bad.

We drove home in silence as, every time I tried to start a sentence, Louise said,

'Nope. Not a word.'

No one was home when we got back, which was a huge relief, as it put off the awful moment of confession. In a cold panic I drove the injured car around to an old barn at the back of the house and opened the doors; it was empty.

'What are you doing?' Louise asked.

I'm going to leave it here for the moment.' I answered.

'Why?' She said 'You're not going to hide it, surely? Honestly, you've got to face her at some stage.'

'I know, but it will give me time to think.' I said, by now my mind was roiling and any happy future dissolving.

When Louise had walked away, deeply disappointed in me, I threw some hay over the worst of the damage, an old guerrilla trick, and went back to the house to join her.

I had no further plan.

When Ali got home, he asked me how the golf had gone.

I was non-committal but said I had something to show him.

I walked him around to the barn, he in some confusion, and threw open the doors. When he saw the car he didn't really understand why it was in the barn covered in straw. He looked at me questioningly.

'And it's what?' He held up his hands.

'It's your mother's car. I said.

'How do you mean?' He asked.

'It's your mother's new car.' I expanded.

'How do you mean?' He repeated.

'It's your mother's new car that was delivered this morning.' I said, quite loudly, pointing at it.

'All right, all right', he said, 'keep your hair on.' And then he looked back at the car, still uncomprehending, and asked,

'Well what is it doing in the barn and why has it got a huge hole in it?'

'That's what I brought you out here to discuss.'

He looked at the car and swept some hay from it, muttered shit a few times, and then he looked back at me. A glimmer of understanding began to spread over his face.

'Oh no, oh no, oh no, oh no you didn't? You couldn't have. Oh for fuck's sake how, why, where?....Oh, no no no no.' He said dropping down onto his haunches and making it difficult for me to answer.

'Do you think she'll mind?' I was looking for any scrap of solace.

'Mind!? Mind!?' He shouted. 'Are you fucking mad, she'll go berserk.'

'Berserk, you think?' I asked quietly but I knew he was right.

Finally, he settled down a bit and stood in melancholy silence.

'What happened?' He whispered.

I explained about his car not starting...

'Not my fault.' he said

....and therefore having to take his mother's car..

'Cunt.' He said.

.....and missing the golf,

'Don't give a shit.' He said.

.....how incredibly unlucky it was that the truck was just there......

'Cunt.' He said again.

.....and that the truck driver had just disappeared......

'Cunt.' He said yet again, but perhaps he meant the truck driver this time. I didn't like to ask.

I concluded the sorry tale.

'And so I thought it would be best to park it here while we decided what to do.'

'Who's we?' He said and I could see which way this was going.

We were both as nervous as each other about his mother's reaction. I pointed out that we were grown men, for heaven's sake, and these things happened, but he merely rolled his eyes. I understood his point.

We discussed many possible ways of dealing with it but they were all either impractical, his, or facetious, mine.

I was the perpetrator, but he was her son so, as I pointed out to him, I could run away but he couldn't, unless he never went home again.

But it turned out his mother wasn't going to be back until after lunch the next day and, as my life was lived from moment to moment in those days, I suggested that we had a drink to stimulate our brains and then a plan was bound to occur to us.

It didn't but we did have a very jolly evening.

The next morning before we went off to play golf, we swore Louise to secrecy in case, by some terrible chance, Ali's mother returned early.

She was rightly deeply resistant to this.

His mother did return early and asked Louise questions that made untruths by omission unavoidable. This took her years to forgive me for; indeed, I'm not sure she ever has.

We got back from our golf to find Ali's mother already home but I still hadn't come up with even the inkling of a plan.

I was all for headlong flight.

But I had to confess.

I couched it in a way that put the blame pretty firmly on the truck driver who, I said, had screeched to a halt and then 'just driven off'. She eyed me suspiciously and mentioned insurance but, as I had no licence and was therefore uninsured, I sabotaged that line of thought quickly.

With my nerves jangling, I took her off to the barn to see her new car for the first time. It was still covered in hay but the hole in the bonnet seemed to have become larger.

She walked around the broken car, picking off the straw and minutely examining every scratch and dent. It looked worse by the second. Occasionally she looked up at me slowly shaking her head with deep disappointment; all her worst suspicions confirmed.

I had let myself down yet again.

She stopped and asked.

I'm not sure I said you could borrow it.'

'Mmm. No, I'm not completely sure you did.' I said, trying to look as if I was casting my mind back.

'No.' She said, now stalking around the back of the car.

'Why the straw?' She asked, pointing at the little left that she hadn't cleared away.

'Well,' I cast around for a un-incriminating answer. 'I thought there might be an oil leak or even petrol and the straw would.....' She interrupted me.

'Go up in flames?' She said.

'Ah, yes, well. Bad idea.' I answered.

In the silence that followed, I said, magnanimously. 'Of course, I will pay for it to be mended.'

During yet another tense longueur that followed, Louise gave me a very old-fashioned look, Ali gave me an incredulous glance and, as his mother opened her mouth, I added.

'In fact, I will buy you a new one.'

Ali said, 'But you haven't got any money.'

And Louise added, 'No you haven't.'

I shrugged in an attempt at insouciance. 'Well, I'll just have to get some.'

Everyone groaned.

EPILOGUE I took the car back to London to have it repaired and parked it outside Ali's flat.

The next morning I went round to take it to the garage and took his then girlfriend, Laura, as my navigator. I reversed straight into a lamp post and badly damaged the rear of the car less than two days after I had destroyed the front.

She, wisely, refused to go any further and took over at the wheel.

This was a baleful episode. My reputation as a driver was shattered and I had behaved appallingly badly throughout but I was probably not as disappointed with myself as I should have been.

Louise insists that I never made good the damage, but I maintain that I did and so we have agreed to differ and, as it is more than forty years on, I feel I have served my time.

She certainly has.

Ali's mother could never look at me again without a slight shudder. Louise brought up this episode if I ever went near a car from then on, but Ali forgave me within only twenty years, like the true friend he is.

This episode also taught me a very important lesson but, as it happened so many years ago, I have forgotten what it is.

5

THE BOTTOM LINE

One of the rules set by my family, were I to write anything approaching a memoir, was that no sex must rear its head in any of these chapters. This is sound advice, I believe, for any writer whether of fact or fiction, for screen or stage.

For sex can be fabulous and uplifting, sublime and life changing but it can also be disappointing, embarrassing or deeply humiliating; or so I'm told.

Rather like real life for most of us.

But not for all of us.

Of the multitude of farcical things humans can do to make themselves look ridiculous, sex is surely the one with the most potential for truly absurd or comical outcomes and so it seems odd that it is little used to this end in literature.

Anyway, that has been my experience, and I can only apologise retrospectively to anyone who didn't think I took it seriously enough or put my back into it, as it were.

When sex becomes emotionally charged it evolves into something else entirely, of course, but I will leave that to the poets and Freudians.

One of my most painful encounters was with a model/actress, of which there was a profusion in Chelsea at that time, with whom I had long been just friends.

I bumped into her when one of her lightning romances had just finished and she asked me to have a drink with her. We went to a local pub, not her natural habitat at all, and she gave me chapter and verse on all her recent affairs, the iniquity of the men and the depravity of their behaviour.

It was rather a cheering way to spend a couple of hours getting drunk and hearing about all the foibles of a rock'n'roll star and an heroic Hollywood figure and listen to her bringing them down to size.

At the end of this rant, she became rather tearful, and I sensed the evening might become awkward, so I poured us into a taxi and dropped her home. To my surprise, as she got out she asked me to come in and, again to my surprise, I declined.

The next time I ran into her I was shopping for a dinner I was giving at my flat. She asked what I was doing and, having explained how chaotic my dinners were, she insisted she prepare and cook it.

Never one to miss the chance to avoid kitchen work, I said yes. She didn't seem the domestic type at all but, as almost everything I'd bought only needed heating, there seemed to be little risk and most of my friends hardly noticed the food anyway.

She went home to change so I shoved everything in the fridge and opened many bottles of what would have been filthy claret, put the vodka on ice and whiskey on the table.

It was a tiny flat and generally extremely messy, but I knew where everything was. I could find any requested LP or single from a pile the size of Ben Nevis in split seconds and the guitar was always on the window-sill so there was no need for any great order to reign.

She returned and asked me to make myself scarce while she got the dinner ready, so I wandered down to the pub. I may have stayed there longer than I had intended as I returned to the flat to find, not only a couple of the guests had arrived, but that it was spotless. The records had been sleeved and shelved, the kitchen gleamed and even my disgrace of a bedroom looked like one in an expensive hotel.

Those who had arrived were stunned by the tidiness of the flat and the sophistication of the dinner table which displayed things I didn't even know I owned.

By the time all the guests had come and been introduced to what seemed so obviously the hostess, there were questions being asked about her provenance and the seriousness of our relationship.

It was with some trouble that I tried to convince them that I didn't know her well at all and had just bumped into her in the street earlier.

The dinner went swimmingly well and the food was, as food should be, filling and much wine was drunk.

We had the usual singsong after dinner followed by a random playing of records while we all shouted along to the tunes. Everyone put on their own favourite to which they mimed and air guitared to. It was a well-worn path to oblivion and might well have been tedious for a sober newcomer.

I had noticed how little our temporary hostess had drunk and how infrequently she had joined in with the brash behaviour after dinner but I put it out of my mind until she started to clear the table while the party was in full swing.

There was a little resistance from some of the older hands, but by what turned out to be after four o'clock, she had managed to persuade everyone to leave.

I remember thanking her for dinner and trying to explain my friends' baroque behaviour and excusing their lack of refinement when she pushed me onto the sofa from which a piece of wood was sticking up that had escaped from its frame something I'd long meant to repair.

Despite the lack of force in the push, I collapsed towards this piece of wood and, twisting my body round to try and avoid it, ended on my back on the sofa at which stage she immediately fell on top of me.

This took me by surprise as I had sensed only a slightly disapproving froideur up to then.

She began to fumble at my shirt buttons.

I confess that, by this time, I was not grasping things as I might have done in the cold light of sobriety so the next part of that night is a blur.

Some time later, I awoke in what appeared to be an underground shelter of some sort. It was heavily shaded, but I sensed a source of light.

I was also very, very cold.

Aliens? A fruitless kidnapping? The first circle of hell? Where on earth was I? Then, as panic rose, swimming into focus and only inches away from my head, I saw a single piece of ravioli - is that a raviolo? I pondered on the familiarity of this pasta and, looking beyond it, I made out a heavily striated black wall which turned out to be a pile of long-playing records.

Neither of these suggested alien abduction or, indeed, any other sort of kidnapping, so I felt it was safe to raise my head a little and see what other clues I might discover. This was excruciatingly painful but did reveal, after some mental wrangling, that I was lying on the floor, under the very table at which we had dined the night before.

The rest of the carpet-vista became only too familiar, the sprinkled albums, the overflowing ashtrays, the bits of cigarette packets fashioned into plectrums and all the other, familiar detritus from a good dinner party.

I looked down to see if I might have injured myself – not an uncommon event in the aftermath of those sorts of evening – to discover I was naked and that some of my clothes were scattered hither and yon.

As I moved a bit more, I felt the most agonising pain in my buttock.

I was loath to move again from this position, as I had become reasonably comfortable, despite the cold and my headache, but the pain was too insistent.

I tried to make sense of this throbbing. I remembered falling onto the damaged sofa and wondered if that was the cause of the pain. This line of thought brought back the memory of the beginning of the previous night's hideous romantic debacle.

I tried desperately to recall what had come next with increasing embarrassment and remorse but to little avail.

I took stock.

I was naked, not good.

There was no sign of her which might have been good or bad.

I had a terrible hangover and pain in my buttock, not good.

I had lost a few hours during which I had gone from fully clothed on the sofa to naked and in pain under the table, not at all good.

I considered all of this and concluded that the sort of pain I was feeling couldn't have resulted from the sofa fall; it was too direct and unusual.

I shuffled myself out from under the table and the sunlight blasting through the window suggested that it was quite late in the morning.

Still lying on the floor, I moved a hand to the agonising centre of pain in my buttock only to find a completely alien and unfathomable object stuck to my skin.

On further exploration it felt like a piece of paper and, yes it was, secured by a closed safety pin stuck through the flesh of my buttock like a laundry tag.

I was confused.

I tried to undo it, not easy with one hand so I lay on my face to use both hands. Each touch of the pin aggravated the pain and so I decided to remove the pin in the bathroom and just tore the bit of paper off.

I raised myself onto one elbow and looked at it.

On it was written,

'YOU FELL ASLEEP. I WENT HOME.'

6

THE ANNUNCIATION

If you have a natural comedic awareness, your antennae will be highly tuned to the unfolding set-up of a good joke, funny anecdote, pun or just a piece of whimsy.

Emerging sets of circumstances, words or actions that begin to reveal themselves as pregnant with possibility, like the slow building of a flush or a straight in a poker hand, begin to pull at your sleeve and say, 'Follow me'.

Sometimes this hand is busted or develops into a minor hand but, just sometimes, it can become a royal flush.

The trick then is to seize the moment and squeeze every drop out of this comedy Godsend.

Nearly fifty years ago my mother and father were due to fly to Jerusalem where my sister, Claire, was living.

She was married to the Italian cultural attaché and Jerusalem was a very important posting both for Italy and the Vatican.

I was to spend Christmas in England while my parents were in Israel and was much looking forward to a few days with my then girlfriend amongst her wonderful brothers, her sister and various young friends of ours.

Sadly, my father died in November that year and so plans were changed and it fell to me to accompany my grieving mother to stay with my sister in Israel.

My mother was then only 57 so I was not her carer, but she was expecting a level of travel and cosseting no longer available, even in the mid-1970s.

We had been told that the weather would be gently autumnal by English standards, so we were surprised to find it freezing and snowing when we arrived.

It seemed doubly jolly to me, though; a White Christmas in the Holy Land.

My mother didn't agree with my take and started to grumble about having nothing warm to wear and her lack of boots so, in the queue for immigration, I hung back to afford myself some separation.

The world was very much on edge then, especially in the Middle East and Ireland. Nothing much has changed.

When I finally got to the passport control officer, he seemed somewhat baffled that anyone with Irish antecedents and born in Egypt should attempt to travel to Tel Aviv.

I explained that my sister lived in Jerusalem and that her husband was an Italian diplomat.

He had the ubiquitous look of world-weariness and cynicism that all passport officers seem to have.

None of this seemed to impress him at all and I was taken off to an empty waiting room where I was told to sit on a chair, watched over by a handsome Israeli lady-soldier in full battledress and armed to the teeth.

The officer had taken my travelling bag and disappeared, and I knew that my mother would be making a nuisance of herself by the luggage carousel, wondering where I was.

I tried making polite conversation with my guard, but to no response. After another quiet hiatus, two male guards took me to a room where I was asked to take off my clothes while they went through them minutely. I was then handed a gown and, in my pants, taken back to the original room now to be guarded by two ladies..

I felt somewhat vulnerable but, at the same time, found the situation inappropriately erotic in a daydream sort of way so, to quash these thoughts, I began to consider the England cricket team's chances against India in the up-and-coming Test Match.

My reverie was interrupted by the original guard appearing with my clothes which I had to put on while the two guards watched me.

Was that a flirtatious smile, I asked myself?

No, it wasn't.

I exited and greeted my sister, who I hadn't seen since my father's funeral a month before. We were used to much longer gaps between meetings, so our greeting was not as theatrical as many of those being performed around us.

Claire flicked her head, motioning behind to my mother, and rolling her eyes tellingly.

'What on earth took you so long?' Ma then asked peevishly, for she was often peeved.

'I was detained by the guards, Ma.' I said.

'Typical.' She spat out. 'What had you done?'

'Nothing, they were just....' I was cut off by her turning around and walking towards the exit doors.

'Fuck me.' I said to Claire. 'This is going to be fun.'

Claire began to laugh, as I did. A lifetime of this ornery behaviour still hadn't prepared us for its appearance at full throttle.

The next day was Christmas Eve, and we were going to Midnight Mass in the Church of the Nativity in Bethlehem.

It seemed such an extraordinary piece of happenstance, to be standing over the actual place that Jesus was born on actual Christmas Day that I almost felt some sort of strange kismet, a harbinger of a better year to come.

My brother-in-law, Romano, had given up his seats in the front row of the church to allow us to join my sister for this epic event.

Claire had converted to Roman Catholicism at the wish of her husband and so was more versed in what the form at a high church Roman Catholic service was than us very low-church Protestants.

I'm not sure what we were expecting, but I suppose some sort of a carol service combined with incense and exotically clothed priests, perhaps.

Being driven to the church in an Italian diplomatic car through what was then the Jordanian corridor while it snowed outside was a strange trip in itself, but we were astonished by the army of nuns and monks from all over the world, milling about outside in the cold.

They wore every conceivable style of habit, surplice, wimple and smock, it was like an ecumenical fashion show but with no make-up.

We were whipped out of the car to find ourselves in a vestibule full of opulently dressed churchmen, diplomats and a collection of beautifully dressed Italian lay men and women.

Our rather ancient tweeds looked absurdly out of place here amongst the world's snappiest dressers, civilian and ordained.

We were shown to our seats in the front row of a packed and gorgeously decorated basilica full to the gunwales with members of every race. I had fallen into a conversation with a rather seedy looking man who spoke English and he told me that this was the absolute zenith of many monks' and nuns' lives.

Of course, I thought, it would be; to be at midnight mass at Bethlehem on Christmas Eve.

The robes and gravitas of the priests conducting the service hinted at just how easy it must have been to wield the huge influence they still had and strike fear into their humble congregations.

I felt a terrible fraud, having blagged my way into this service, especially not being a Roman Catholic, when so many would have given their eye teeth to have been in my position.

Suddenly, with a thundering blast on the organ, the service started.

Neither my mother nor I, probably the only two protestants in the church, had any idea what to do or indeed when to do it, so we followed the congregation in a religious version of Simple Simon Says. We also had no idea what anyone was chanting, praying or singing so we mouthed along nodding our heads slightly.

What I remember most is that it went on for so long that I was expecting a rock of ages to cleft for me at any moment.

My mother began to nudge me and ask me where the loo was. I pointed out to her that I was unlikely to know where she could spend a penny in the Basilica of the Nativity in Bethlehem so I would ask someone else but then I forgot.

After what seemed hours of chanting and replies, standing up and sitting down, it was communion time.

It soon became apparent that not only was communion about to start but that absolutely everybody both in and around the church was going to be taking it.

I looked at the hordes of people and began to calculate how long it would take to get through this throng and reckoned another hour, at least.

My mother was clearly not going to last that long and I realised that I wouldn't either so we needed a loo.

The celebrants inside were now beginning to return to the back of the church but, just when we thought it was all over, the doors were opened, letting in another army of nuns, monks and priests who had been waiting their turn outside.

Our hearts sank and I was afraid my mother's soul was going to be damned to eternal purgatory for peeing on the floor when she suddenly hurtled towards the open doors like a Fuseli painting of a woman fleeing before the wrath of God which, indeed, she might well have been.

The line of punters seemed endless and there were still many to go when my mother returned, relieved but, strangely, smelling strongly of sherry.

'I found some nice monks.' She said cryptically.

The line was, at last, coming to an end and, as the last communicant made his way back from the rail, we all stood as a mighty organ piece rent the air.

Many prayers were chanted and answered, many more bits of mysterious business took place and then, quite suddenly, it was time to leave.

My heart leapt, I was bursting for a cigarette, a pee, a drink and a cup of coffee, in that order.

As we tried to leave the church, about a dozen of us were corralled into a small side hall by the exit. Then, the cleric who had taken the whole, epic service, shook us each by the hand, smiled, turned and led us down to the bowels of the earth.

My heart sank, the chance for my long-awaited smoke had been snatched away and I groaned inwardly or perhaps outwardly, judging by the look I got from my fellow travellers.

We were taken to a tiny room, like a cave, which was believed to have been where the famous manger had stood all those years ago. I have to say it was a very moving experience and I even lost the overwhelming urge to pee that had assailed me so strongly just seconds before.

Perhaps it was a miracle.

Not a significant one, obviously, but nonetheless....

After a short time gazing at the very spot, we rose again and, feeling much more holy, found ourselves in the square outside the church.

My mother and sister were talking to two Franciscan friars who were kindly going to take us to their place for a short kip followed by them cooking a traditional English Christmas lunch specially for us that they were preparing with the help of an ancient copy of Mrs Beeton's excellent Book of Household Management.

As we had half an hour to kill, I excused myself and found a small café, and ordered a cup of coffee, fresh orange juice and a large brandy.

I asked if they had a telephone that I could use to call England. They pointed to a small cubicle with a stool and an ancient contraption on the wall. They explained that they would book the intercontinental call, a palaver in those days, and a receptionist would call when the line was ready.

I gave them the surname and number of the girlfriend I'd hoped to spend Christmas with.

All international calls in those days were 'person to person' to avoid running up a huge bill talking to the wrong one.

I had calculated that her family should still be at home before going to the Christmas Morning service in their village, so my timing could not have been better.

I settled down with my café and cognac and drew deeply on a cigarette, contemplating the outlandish service I had just witnessed and the bizarre set of circumstances that had led me to Bethlehem on Christmas morning.

I wondered if the Magi had themselves stopped for a smoke and a drink after delivering their presents. The telephone rang in the cubicle.

I opened the door, worked myself into the tiny space, settled onto the seat and picked up the receiver.

The operator was talking to an Englishman through the tinny crackle that then pervaded all intercontinental calls and gave you a real sense of the distance between callers.

'Allo, Sir, allo, Sir.' Said the operator and then asked him if she had the right number and name.

'Yes.' I heard the suave tones of my girlfriend's famously dry and witty brother at the other end of the line.

'That's my name..... how can I help?'

'OK, OK, Sir, I have a person-to-person call for you from Bethlehem.'

Without missing a beat, he said,

'Don't tell me.....it's a boy.'

7

No Boundaries

For many years I stayed with a friend for an annual cricket weekend in Devon where his eclectic eleven played against a local team.

It was a weekend we anticipated with real joy as George's hospitality was always both informal and lavish. There were absolutely no rules and a wonderful time was had by almost everyone.

One of this fixture's great charms was that it attracted a very eccentric and individual team. All of them played for this wandering club often and in every corner of the country but very rarely would more than two or three of us be in a team at the same time. The side was run by an idiosyncratic and brilliant man, James, whose academic feats were legend but who was also, off and on, the world rackets champion and a very useful wicketkeeper and batsman. He was astonishingly lazy, grotesquely unsavoury in his personal habits, habitually rude to almost everybody but also exceptionally funny.

He worked as a sort of human computer for brokers at Lloyd's of London - before the machine versions were invented and made his job all but obsolete. His antiquated and completely original way with words enchanted both me and Louise, who was one of the few women who could see past his off-putting exterior to the kind, clever and wry man beneath.

I suspect that it was James's conceit to find the most reckless team he possibly could, one that could both play decent cricket but also be relied upon to cause incidents.

If this was his ambition, he succeeded admirably. No fixture I ever played in was the scene of so many accidents, misunderstandings or so much laughter.

George was the perfect host for such a collection of misfits. He genuinely didn't care how anybody behaved and hundreds of years in a secluded part of Devon had rendered his family impervious to what others thought.

One of our team, Rupert, whose name couldn't have less suited his huge, gangling figure and twitching, permanently bemused face, spoke so loudly out of the side of his mouth that it was often hard to follow his speech let alone his train of thought. He laughed manically a great deal at almost anything and his lack of physical coordination made his every approach to the wicket as he ran in to bowl a potential disaster.

To those who didn't know him, Rupert could be a terrifying sight merely sitting down but, in full, flailing form, he was Beelzebub's hitman.

Walking down a village lane in rural backwaters, where we often played, the locals cowered behind their curtains until he was out of sight.

I would usually get a lift down with Ali as the least mad option as the team shared three cars. One's passengers consisted of a man who spoke in figures and could only be understood by James, a short and gurning bald man who laughed so hard and so bizarrely at simply anything that he eventually induced hysteria in even the most serious people, and a landscape gardener. Another carried an ex-county cricket captain who owned a massage parlour in the King's Road, a listless but droll, middle-aged man who was almost the last living flâneur and a couple of good and immensely jolly players, who were nice enough to be able to put up with the others.

These were our team.

James travelled alone as his antique car was genuinely unsanitary and filled with so many inexplicable and revolting objects that he very rarely had a passenger.

I was once behind him at an airport on a Middle Eastern tour when an unsuspecting customs lady asked him to reveal the contents of his cricket bag, a piece of luggage of a shape she would never have seen.

We all cried out, trying to dissuade her, as nothing within had been given so much as the vaguest wash for a decade or more, but this just made her even more inquisitive. He obliged and this unfortunate lady took a step back, like a heroine in a melodrama being confronted with a dead body, as he pulled its sides open.

The smell that emanated from this toxic bag was quite bad enough, but the brave girl put her hand inside and rummaged around, holding her breath with her head held well back and pulled out, of all things, his odious and miscoloured gentleman's abdominal protector.

As she held it up with a baffled look, shrugging her shoulders, it became obvious she didn't speak English so we helpfully called out words like 'shield' and 'protection' at which stage she lifted the wretched, triangular object towards her face which, on reflection, would seem the obvious place for it to be worn if you didn't actually know. Just in time, we let out such a collective gasp of horror - as a pantomime audience would have if she were about to put her hand into a snake-pit – that she shrieked and dropped it before it could sully her.

She moved away from his bag while James, crying and screeching out his high-pitched giggle, retrieved his 'box'. She quickly waved us all through.

James liked to win at all costs but nevertheless chose his team of disparate players knowing none of us cared nearly as much as he did. This was part of his overall plan. He wanted to beat the opposition, despite his obviously bizarre team, on guile and what he considered strategic leadership and what we considered gamesmanship.

In his own, rarefied world, this sweetened the victory.

The game always took place at a ground that had a small and threatening section of the boundary only separated from a cliff top by a short stretch of long grass.

There were concrete posts marking this hazard every few yards and there had, at one stage, been steel wire running through the holes in them to stop deep fielders making lemming-like mistakes. This wire had broken in many places and those sections now lay threading dangerously and invisibly through the grass.

It was, anyway, assumed that nobody in their right mind would chase a ball even up to, let alone beyond, the boundary for the very real risk of disappearing over the cliff.

However, this theory had not been tested on the erratic behaviour of our team.

Most of the rest of the boundary ran into beautiful little sand dunes some of them, though not those in front of the cliff, alive with stinging nettles.

The pavilion was picturesque, an Edwardian thatched building and this annual fixture used to gather quite a large audience as it was always highly entertaining. The cricket was of a decent standard and the food and drink were exceptionally good.

It was obvious that the game itself had become a mere sideshow to watching Rupert and many locals would turn up to see the comedic sight of his ungainly form running and floundering, emitting huge grunts or shouting unsolicited appeals from the boundary.

Among the spectators there were also some baser elements, there for the now traditional accidents in which he was so often involved. These crowds grew every year, like gladiatorial audiences, as word spread that the inevitable tragedy must one day unfold when Rupert finally disappeared over the cliff.

This eventuality was encouraged by James who always positioned Rupert where he would most often have to run towards the treacherous boundary, however unnecessary that position might be.

Over the years there had been many, but minor, mishaps. Rupert had often tripped during his run up or splayed himself heavily on the square as the final lunge of his follow-through became too much for his bulk. The noise that burst out of him when this happened would bring gasps, and even applause, from the audience.

He had also, too often, run into other fielders while going for their catch, causing terrible clashes and, more often than any other cricketer I have ever seen, fallen onto the stumps, nearly impaling himself.

He once chased a ball to the boundary, some yards from the cliff zone but nonetheless in the nettle zone, become entangled in the wire and fallen headfirst into the very deepest part of the nettlebed.

There was a brooding silence.

Even that hardened audience let out a collective gasp of sympathy as Rupert completely vanished.

Only the distant call of the seagulls and the waves broke the silence until, with a mighty roar, he leapt up slapping himself. Then he stopped, picked up the ball and rushed forwards hurling it towards the pavilion and then running after it shouting horrible oaths.

It was obvious that he had been terribly stung and, as he neared the spectators, they saw that his face had swollen and become blotched as if he had a terrible case of measles. He continued running up the pavilion steps and into the changing room while someone, who seemed to have some first aid experience, trotted after him.

But, before they could catch up with him, he emerged holding not the bottle of healing balm we were expecting, but a bottle of gin from which he took two or three long swigs, placed it back on the ground and ran back to his position on the field.

He made no reference to it again that day and, when asked how he was feeling, looked back at his inquisitor baffled.

It was a few years later that the inevitable happened.

James had, by this time, placed Rupert in various vulnerable positions in the field hoping that one day it would pay off. I believe his hope was for some very high-quality and well-planned slapstick as payment for his patience but the dénouement, when it came, took us all by surprise.

Rupert had bowled a few energetic and eventful overs and was now fielding, facing the batsman, beyond and to the side of the bowler, at what is called mid-off. The ball was driven sweetly and, as it sped to the side of him, Rupert turned to give chase.

Even his biggest fan wouldn't have put money on his ever getting to the ball but, like the great warhorse he was, he did not give up.

Just short of the cliff boundary, it looked as if he was going to throw himself headlong at the ball but, at the last moment, he jumped after it in the hope of back-heeling it before it went over the line.

Sadly, his mighty leap only took him as far as the ball and he landed on it, turned over his ankle and was thrown, headlong towards the cliff.

The crowd held its breath and even his teammates, all of whom had seen him survive some terrible accidents, thought that the time had come to meet his maker - whoever that could possibly have been.

As he shot forward towards what many of us assumed would be his last breath, there were others of us - who had witnessed the savagery his body had survived over the years - who wondered if he might not be the only man alive able to withstand a three-hundred-foot fall onto rocks.

There was a sudden, terrible crack like a bullwhip, drawing a huge exhalation of breath from the crowd and a truly bestial bellow from Rupert as his forward momentum was suddenly arrested.

He became inert for a moment but then appeared to bounce back from the concrete post whose corner he had hit full on with the middle of his forehead.

Even the most battle-hardened of us realised that this was a truly terrible accident.

We rushed towards him.

Even James, who I had never actually seen running before, broke into a trot as we neared the prone and groaning figure.

There was a mighty plum-coloured gash running from between his eyes up through the entirety of his forehead to above his hairline.

He was moaning like a birthing cow.

Helpfully, one of our team said, 'Raise his feet to staunch the flow of blood!'

He was then given a series of tutting investigations by people completely unversed in first aid as they got close enough to inspect the appalling damage.

Rupert had followed the spurious raised-leg advice, so we pushed the legs back down again. Theories of what to do abounded and were shouted down by ever more unlikely theories.

Someone had mercifully rung for an ambulance and, as there wasn't a doctor in the house, two people were running across the pitch towards us who turned out to be a vet and a nurse.

They introduced themselves as they squatted down beside the prone figure and there were some inappropriate remarks about the vet probably being of more use when James, peering closely into Rupert's wound, suddenly cried out, in his strange falsetto voice,

'Good God, would you believe it!?'

'What?' we all said.

'I can see his brain,' shouted James.

'Really?' We cried out.

'Yes, and there's something here,' he continued. 'My God, it's some words.'

'It's what?' We cried, even louder peering towards the suppurating wound.

'It's a message.' He said, squinting.

'What does it say?' We cried as one.

'Hang on, it says....' and here he peered even closer 'Not to be used after 1964.'

I'm ashamed to say we all laughed.

So it was that these two worthy citizens who had offered their help, watched us all trying now to suppress our laughter as our friend lay groaning, badly wounded, on the ground, his eyes beginning to sport purple aureoles as a huge bruise raised itself the length of the gash.

When Rupert asked, 'How does it look?' no one was brave enough to answer except James, who said,

'There is nothing in the animal kingdom to which I can compare the way your face now looks, Rupert old friend. It is *sui generis*, a thing doctors and scientists will discuss to the end of time. In short it is simply horrible.'

'What did he say.' He asked and so I translated.

'Not good, I'm afraid.'

The nurse person had taken the two flaps of the wound and was pushing them together when an ambulance raced over the pitch.

It had come remarkably quickly and they bundled Rupert onto a stretcher, driving him off to hospital.

We took an early tea and discussed what we thought the outcome might be.

We were amazed that he had survived at all and that the right angle of the concrete post that he had hit at full tilt hadn't killed him outright. This extraordinary escape led us all to believe that he would probably survive and that, anyway, any change to his brain could only be for the better.

I asked James if this endpiece to his strategy of so many years had been satisfying and he said it was more than he could possibly have hoped for. He added that, although the flight over the cliff would have been a pure and thrilling dénouement, the almost certain expectation of that happening being suddenly substituted for a possibly even more appalling end, had given an extra frisson to the whole thing.

I understood that James was merely playing his part in the faux-unfeeling conversations we often had and, in fact he was very shaken and asked regularly for updates on Rupert.

He'd been taken to a nearby hospital, stitched up and, we learnt, was on concussion watch, having his vital signs monitored so, as soon as the game was over, we piled into various cars to go and see how he was.

We arrived at the hospital to find things in some disarray.

The nurses told us that he had been heavily concussed and making little sense. He'd had many stitches and was meant to be under observation, but he'd dismissed himself and plunged noisily out of the hospital towards the town.

We deduced that he couldn't have gone far and that his likely destination would be the nearest pub but we also guessed he would have had no money on him and worried that things might have got a bit complicated if that was indeed where he had gone.

We looked through the window of the first pub we came across and saw no sign of him but one of us went in to look anyway.

He reported that Rupert had indeed been in and that the regulars had been terrified by the sight of him. As he had no money on him he'd asked someone to stand him a drink but the brave barman had asked him to leave.

Our informant added that the man who'd given him this news had crossed himself during the telling.

The second pub's regulars clearly had more stomach than the first as we discovered Rupert surrounded by a rapt audience and a host of drinks, bellowing out a completely fantastical story about what had happened to him.

The time that had passed since we'd last seen him had not been kind to him.

He had obviously taken off any dressing the hospital had put over the livid, glistening wound. It had umpteen thick stitches binding it together and the skin showed a spectrum of purple around the wound graduating to a jaundiced yellow at the extremities of his face. He had two very bruised sockets under his black, bushy eyebrows and very bloodshot, demonic eyeballs.

They had shaved back the front inch or so of his hairline to allow the stitches to continue above his forehead which made him look like Frankenstein's monster's much more sinister brother.

We reckoned that, had he gone into a less urbane rural pub, he might have had a stake driven through his heart or been set on fire.

We drove him home and took turns in keeping him awake as the nurses had instructed us. They had commanded that we shouldn't let him fall asleep until we were quite sure he was not impaired by his accident.

Being Rupert, this was difficult to judge.

Eventually we gave up trying and the next morning he rose like Lazarus and took the field to mighty cheers from the biggest crowd we had ever had there, encouraged by the episode of the day before and secretly hoping for an encore.

James had had enough fun and moved Rupert to the pavilion end where he stood like some huge, maimed beast and, mercifully, came to no more harm.

8

A Shot In the Dark

The following year we all reappeared believing that the worst must be past and that we might well have an accident-free weekend. Rupert appeared with a girlfriend who was very handsome, very tall and very, very thirsty. He went on to marry this Amazonian figure who James christened, 'Stay, for the night is young, and I am enormous.'

Rupert didn't feature in that year's drama and nor did it happen on the cricket pitch.

Our host, George, had an absolute fetish for guns, weaponry, old war films and all things boyishly dangerous.

Many boys have such a phase in their early youth but George's had remained. In the days when guns weren't so much associated with criminality, old ones from the various wars in which members of a family might have taken part, could find themselves secreted around a house along with dress swords, daggers and other pieces of weaponry some, perhaps, even taken off His or Her Majesty's enemies.

Sometimes, added to these, were weapons that had been swapped for something else and, until the great amnesties during which millions of guns and weapons were handed in to the police, any vaguely military family might have held on to a few of these bits of lethal memorabilia.

One evening, George informed us, after a very long dinner, that he owned a terrific Spanish pistol that shot six rounds at breathtaking speed and accuracy.

By the time he announced this, there were only three of us still up, Ali being the third. George decided that now would be a good time to demonstrate the brilliance of this pistol.

'Why then, at two in the morning?' you might ask, and I can honestly give you no sensible answer.

We went out into the darkness and George set up six empty tins on a wall about three foot high behind the house by some barns which had another wall behind them; so far this all seemed fairly sensible.

We stood behind him, responsibly, and he said 'Watch this'.

He pulled the trigger and counted, 'One, two, three...' and so on.

After he called each number, came the almighty bang of the gun being fired followed by no noise of any of the cans even moving but just a slightly disconcerting hum of the ricocheting rounds disappearing into the darkness.

After he had said 'six' and the last bullet had been fired, he dropped the hand holding the gun down by his side and, as it reached its nadir, there was another loud bang.

To our collective surprise, the gun actually held seven rounds.

George stumbled a little. Ali and I looked at each other.

Our first thought was, I believe, 'Silly arse, that could have been nasty.'

And then George took another lurch forward and said, 'Christ, I've shot myself.'

We assumed this was a joke in rather bad taste so we giggled nervously but then he clutched his right leg and said.

'No, really'

It was dark, and very difficult to see anything at all, so I lit my cigarette lighter and there was, indeed, a small round hole in his trousers, just above the knee.

'Ouch.' He said.

'Does it sting?' Asked Ali.

'Yes, it really does.' Said George, not unsurprisingly.

At that moment Louise opened the bedroom window and asked, 'What the fuck are you doing?'

Looking up, I said, 'George just shot himself in the leg.'

'Christ, you idiots.' She said and closed the window.

'Fuck, we better get you to hospital.' Ali said 'Do you think you can drive?'

'He's got a bullet in his leg, of course he can't drive.' I pointed out.

'Well, you can't drive at all so......'

'You're going to have to drive, Ali.' Said George.

We put one of his arms over each of our shoulders and took him to the front of the house and laid him in the back of Ali's car.

The drive to the hospital was made even more challenging by the state of the driver and, years before satnav, the prone position of the wounded man on the back seat who, though extraordinarily stoic, was unable to see the roads well enough to guide us so there were many wrong turns on the dark and hedgerowed Devonian country lane.

When we got to the final turning, Ali and I discussed performing the classic gun-wounded man-hospital-drop-off scenario we had seen so often in films. A car roars into the hospital forecourt, where the victim is pushed, rolling out onto the hospital steps while the car that brought him screeches off into the night with its door still flapping open as a couple of hospital workers rush out, look down at the injured man, and then look up at the disappearing car in confusion.

George said this wouldn't be necessary as we were in Taunton.

Finally, after some confusion as to which road was the one for the main hospital, which was the maternity wing and which went to A&E, we pulled up and got the wounded man up the steps and into the hospital.

Ali and I were extremely worried that the bullet might have gone through his knee, causing some serious and permanent damage.

There was very little blood but none of us knew if that was a good or a bad thing.

A nurse asked what had happened and we all tried to explain at once.

'Have you been drinking?' She said, looking suspiciously at all three of us.

We remained silent.

Then Ali said,

'Num.'

Before we could take this conversation much further, a doctor arrived.

He was middle-aged and reassuring and, it transpired, had been with the military in Malaya as a medic and had seen and dealt with bullet wounds before. 'What are the chances?' We all said, rather too light-heartedly for what was obviously not a humorous situation.

This was made even less so by the fact that it seemed bullet wounds were taken very seriously indeed in Devon.

Our slightly conflicting versions of the episode were not helping matters when the doctor held up his hand and asked George how he had come by this wound.

I have to say I was very impressed by George's sang-froid as he told him the story, to the letter, of exactly what had happened.

On reflection, the whole event did seem somewhat asinine and, to an overworked A&E doctor at three in the morning, considerably more than that.

'I shall have to tell the police.' He said as he studied George's leg.

'Why? No one got hurt and it was self-inflicted...'

He gave us a very hard look which seemed to say, I've seen lots of people like you before and you are a waste of space. I am a doctor, and I am useful.

'The law, I'm afraid.' He said and we did begin to feel like we were in a movie, albeit a black and white, British, 1950s B-film in which George would have said, at this stage, 'It's a fair cop.'

They took the wounded man off on a gurney and we sat down in the waiting area to have a cigarette in the waiting room; an extraordinary idea now.

As we waited, we discussed how lamentably unprepared we both were for the battlefield and how appalling our lack of emergency medical knowledge was. We were just pledging to take first-aid lessons on Monday and make ourselves battlefield fit when the doctor returned.

He had been impressively quick.

'He's been very lucky, indeed.' He almost smiled. 'Bullet still in there, took it out, went along under the skin, cut it open, cleaned him out, stitched him up, should be fine.'

We thanked him profusely and he told us we should leave as George would need to stay overnight.

As it happened, and quite by chance, we also left before the authorities had arrived.

We got back to a sleeping house but, as people began to wake up and ask after George, we found ourselves being condemned for encouraging the tomfoolery that had led to his wound rather than being thanked for taking him to the hospital.

Both Ali and I felt somewhat hard done by, as we had been innocent bystanders, but their point was very well made by a rather annoying legal man at breakfast. We had aided and abetted George, he opined, simply by not stopping him as any sensible person would have done.

There was an obvious flaw in this argument, but I took another tack.

'It's George's house....so it was difficult to tell him what he could and couldn't do.' I offered.

'Aha,' said the QC in that way they do, 'so if you had seen George pouring petrol on the house and taking out some matches, you wouldn't have stopped him? Good manners would have prevailed?'

I paused too long.

It gave everyone a chance to say things like 'Quite right,' and 'Well, said.'

The collection of irresponsible and lawless people around the table had suddenly become perfect, model citizens.

'Anyway,' I said, I made another mistimed pause. 'Anyway what?' Said the QC.

'Just anyway.' I said which didn't exactly win the argument but left room for doubt, I thought.

George came back, later in the day, little the worse for wear and with a genuine bullet scar, something I'm sure he had often dreamt of having, as a conversation piece for when future conversations might be flagging.

This absurd incident was really the acme of the Devon follies and, although there were more minor accidents and injuries, none ever reached the hights of Rupert's argument with the concrete post or George's shot in the dark.

The final year that I played, an old rustic wandered over to me as I was fielding on the boundary and, with a wistful look over the cliff, said.

'Not the same as it was in Rupert's day. Now he really was worth watching.'

I had to agree with him.

9

EYE OFF THE BALL

It was a glorious spring day and all was right with the world. I was in my early twenties and, for reasons I can't recall, feeling chipper and somewhat pleased with myself as I walked towards the King's Road.

It was the early 1970s and a walk towards that fabled road was always joyful then.

I skipped into the playground behind St Luke's Church to take a shortcut and there, walking towards me, was one of the prettiest girls I had ever seen. She was walking slowly, propping up a very old, painfully thin and delicate looking lady; her grandmother I supposed.

Despite her great age, the old girl had a wonderfully fresh and kind face and her aura signalled that, even if she only had a few years left to her, she was going to enjoy every second and the way she looked at the beautiful creature on her arm, signalled that there was simply no-one else she would rather spend them with.

It was a scene that filled my heart with love for the world and I remember beaming with goodwill at humanity in general but, especially at this adorable couple.

The young goddess looked up as I neared them and, seeing me grinning so happily, politely smiled back. This prompted the old girl to look up and also smile at me smiling at her and then she smiled up at her young minder who was now smiling at me smiling at her. We were all now smiling at each other and fun and laughter was in the air.

As this smile fest was in full swing, some lads who had been playing a noisy kickabout game of soccer behind my heart's desire, kicked a ball over the top of the two ladies and it bobbled its erratic way towards me.

So full of the joys of spring was I that a ball wending its way to me was as irresistible as a ripe plum on a tree and offered me the chance to show off a little bit.

I would boot the ball miles into the air, eliciting gasps from all the walkers in the garden, especially the two ladies, and then smile with a modesty and insouciance that would be beguiling, if not to the younger lady, then to the older one who might, anyway, be the gatekeeper to her heart.

I mused how, in days to come, the story of where we first met and how impressed granny had been with my sporting prowess and the laughter we all shared afterwards would become a fable in our conjoined families.

How I stopped to talk and then help them across the road would complete this legend of which no-one would ever tire.

The football was nearing me, and I surmised, from its scratchy and erratic bounce, that it was one of those very light plastic ones that don't always behave as consistently as their somewhat heavier and better made leather cousins.

'These light ones need a really solid kick to go any impressive distance.' I thought to myself.

I was still smiling, as were the two ladies, and a moment of expectancy had bestilled this little tableau in that tiny park.

The boys whose ball it was were watching expectantly, also smiling, awaiting the return of their ball and casual walkers looked over their shoulders to savour the moment.

A benign and smiley sense of anticipation stilled the air as I stepped forward to lash out at the ball.

Being light, it bounced slightly awkwardly and, instead of meeting my instep for the classic punt that I had set myself up for, it came off the outside of my foot like bullet with a loud wheezing noise and flew hard and fast straight towards the old lady's head.

I was only a few feet away from her by now and it hit her square in the face with a terrible, loud slapping noise and, by chance, ricocheted off towards the boys who owned the ball.

'Cheers.' One of them said thoughtlessly.

'Nice work.' Said another.

The old dear dropped to the path like a stone, taking the young girl with whose arm she was entangled down with her.

They both lay, stunned, on the ground.

Blood had burst from her ancient nose and her top lip had begun to swell alarmingly. Her eyes, even more worryingly, were closed and she appeared lifeless.

I was wondering what I might do to retrieve the situation and claw my way back into their good books (the reel running the romantic film in my mind had suddenly come undone and the loose spool was flapping wildly) when an efficient looking man in rimless glasses moved towards us.

He announced, self-importantly, that he was a doctor from the Brompton Hospital which was just over the road, and immediately took charge.

'You,' he said to me, 'go over to the hospital and get them to send someone over with a stretcher.'

'But...' I answered.

'What are you waiting for?' He said, 'Is that not clear?'

I turned to do his bidding.

'Is that a clean handkerchief?' He added as I walked away.

I nodded as he put his hand out.

I hesitated just a fraction.

The young girl looked at me with some disdain.

'Come on then, hand it over, for God's sake, she's bleeding.' He said and the girl grabbed it from my top pocket before I had a chance to act and shook her head at me.

'Honestly,' she said, 'what's wrong with you? Go and get the stretcher people.' She looked at me with something way beyond disdain this time.

'Someone's already gone to get the stretcher team.' Said someone.

'Thank God someone's prepared to help.' She said with a flick of her lovely head.

The old lady was beginning to come to, so at least the spectre of murder or homicide was receding,

'Does she wear dentures.' The doctor asked, which seemed unnecessarily personal.

'False teeth, Granny?' the girl mused, 'Yes…yes I think she does.'

'Aha.' I said loudly without meaning to, 'So she *is* your Granny.'

'Yes. What's that got to do with anything? You've almost killed her so if you can't help just fuck off.'

Everyone stopped whatever they were doing and became still.

It seemed such an unlikely sentence to have come from her lovely mouth and so loudly, too.

After a short hiatus, the assembled crowd began to move around again and, to a person, they looked at me coldly.

I had forced this virginal mouth to desecrate itself, their gaze seemed to say.

The doctor had got his fingers into granny's mouth and was pulling out her false teeth. This made her look even more vulnerable and shockingly cadaverous and she had so lost her bloom that her granddaughter was now whimpering.

The stretcher team arrived and began to dab at her face and make her comfortable. She opened her eyes for the first time since the ball had struck her. She noticed her smiling granddaughter and tried to smile back but this obviously hurt as she gave a little wince. This attempted smile obviously alerted her to her lack of teeth for she covered her lower face with her hand in a gesture of heart-breaking embarrassment.

As she was being tucked into the stretcher, she glanced over to me and I tried to smile reassuringly at her while mouthing the words 'I'm so sorry'.

What she mistook this for I will never know but the look she gave me back and the ungodly croak that hacked from her toothless mouth sounded like a curse of eternal damnation from a more than usually angry Hecate.

The beautiful girl stood up and moved off with the stretcher. The old girl had closed her eyes and seemed more at peace now that she had consigned me to a terrible fate.

The doctor had wrapped her teeth in my handkerchief, and I saw an opportunity.

'Do you want me to look after those?' I asked the doctor, now walking beside the girl and reassuring her.

'Look after what?' he asked, and the girl turned around to look at me.

'Her teeth.' I explained.

'Why on earth should you do that?' The doctor said with some reason.

'Just a thought.' I said.

'What is wrong with you?' The girl asked.

'Just trying to help.' I tried to look hard done by.

'Why don't you just go away?' She said, 'You've done quite enough damage and we really don't need you anymore.'

Our progress was being closely watched by the many walkers who made a clearing along the short distance to the gate almost all of whom had witnessed the unfortunate incident and it was only too apparent that I was very much the villain of the piece.

The only people vaguely on my side appeared to be the owners of the ball as these urchins seemed to see much comedy in the situation.

The rest of the crowd were in a hanging mood.

The young Venus stopped, causing the doctor to come to a halt also, turned around and said, loudly.

'Will you stop following me!?'

The crowd began to murmur and moved menacingly towards me. They were turning ugly.

I was not a brave young man but I walked over to her and said.

'Look, I'm so sorry, it was all a ghastly mistake, really, an accident.'

And I threw myself on her mercy.

'You and your granny looked so wonderful together that I was trying to impress you by kicking the ball. It was just a terrible.....'

My voice petered out, I couldn't read her expression at all.

Was that a hint of sympathy crossing over that lovely face?

No, it wasn't.

'Impress us by kicking a ball?' She asked and I could see it wasn't quite what a knight errant might offer.

'What are you talking about?' She said and followed this with an even louder,

'Will you please just fuck off!?

'Ooooooo!' went the crowd.

As she turned to leave, I called out.

'Can I have you're telephone number?'

And even her granny tried to raise herself to look at me after this brazen request.

The crowd sucked in its breath.

'Are you completely bonkers, are you mad?' She said, 'Why in a million years would I give you my number?'

'So I can check up on your grandmother and see how she is.' I said, trying to look broken and penitent.

'No you bloody well can't' she hissed, 'I never want to see you again.'

It seemed pretty final so I said - and I've always regretted this,

'Can I have my hanky back, then?'

10

A Test of Nerves

I have never actually passed a driving test or possessed a full driving licence. This may not come as much of a surprise to those who have driven with me or allowed me to drive their cars.

For some years, before I was married, I drove on a provisional licence, never really appreciating the seriousness of what I was doing.

I genuinely thought that a driver's licence was no more important than, say, a dog licence and its absence would only result in a telling off from the Old Bill, were I apprehended.

When Louise discovered my licence was merely provisional, she forbade me from ever driving again and, except for an unsuccessful driving lesson a few years ago that changed my instructor's views on his vocation, I haven't driven a car for decades.

My careless driving took place mainly during the highway's salad days when the roads were far less congested, seat belts were not compulsory, there were no speed limits, few breathalysers and many people drove appallingly badly. The obvious drawback to this relaxed state of affairs was that, even though the British roads were comparatively empty as there was only one car for every eight now, there were nearly five times as many deaths on the roads as there are now.

Good Lord, I hear you say, and you would be right, because pro rata it would mean 64,000 deaths on our roads today. For fans of stats, this is one of the most extraordinary and salutary and may even be accurate. The reasons for the previous carnage were many; cars were less safe and technologically vastly inferior (so I am told), and none of the other life-saving regulations had been imposed. There are also far more people travelling on motorways now which, counterintuitively, is the safest way to travel and, importantly, there are far fewer inept idiots like me driving about.

I did once take my test in Malton, a small town in Yorkshire, as it was then famous for never failing anyone who could even open a car door.

I'd had the vaguest of lessons from my father who had learnt as he went along in the army but he considered himself a natural driver and, if that were judged by travelling very fast with hope in your heart, he was.

He gave up on me almost immediately saying I had no empathy for a motor car. He himself was no stranger to car crashes – shunts to him - of which he had many all over the world. He actually gave up drinking after a nearly disastrous muddle, as he called it, with a van very late at night on his way back from the York races.

The local police knew him - not in a professional way - so, as no real damage had been done and nobody was more than scratched, he was taken home by the rozzers and nothing more was said.

He was so appalled by how close he had come to a serious accident and injuring, or even worse, innocent people, that he sentenced himself to a year off the roads and gave up drinking. It was a very unusual, self-inflicted penance but a typical overreaction from him and showed the Quaker streak he tried so hard to hide.

I was very occasionally allowed to drive my mother's box-shaped Ford Popular around the local roads while she shouted incomprehensible instructions at me. These cars were known as 'sit up and begs' for their shape, a distinctly inappropriate motor for my mother whose more typical position was slouched by the Dubonnet bottle taking no shit from anyone.

She was an indescribably bad driver herself, having learnt informally during the war. For a short time she drove a general around very sedately in a staff car in London and then, bored of that, she drove an ambulance in Coventry during their terrible bombing.

Like many of her age and background, she did very brave things that she never mentioned, and it was only talking to one of her wartime co-drivers that I gathered just how dangerous and terrifying it had been and just how courageously she had behaved.

I think the trauma caused by what she, and women like her, had seen and had to deal with in the war, without ever being able to discuss it, went a long way to explaining why so many of them seemed emotionally distant - and developed an over-enthusiasm for cocktails.

This training had given her a taste for driving fast, as you had to under those terrifying conditions, steering around craters and unexpected vehicles on a road lit only by fires and falling bombs. Even though those conditions very rarely occurred on the A1 north of Sandy, it was no less stressful driving along narrow Yorkshire lanes with my mother behind the wheel.

She had a badge in the shape of a V, which had a small disc and held a number that represented the years its owner had driven without a crash. She was inordinately proud of this. She never admitted to having had a crash so as not to lose her unstained record and number, which was 64 by the time she last graced the highways. I had been in a car with her many times when she had a shunt but she would never admit to anything being her fault or claim on her insurance so as not to lose her score on this wretched badge.

Her role in these accidents was as a sort of highway *agent provocateur*, causing other people to crash by her unexpected, impromptu manoeuvres.

She would draw to a sudden stop with no warning and then move on, leaving the poor person following floundering and often having to hit something to avoid her. She would pull out into country roads only ever looking one way and shout,

'What on Earth does he think he's doing?' As some poor person, forced to avoid her, hit the hedgerow.

'Honestly, why are these people allowed on the roads if they can't drive?' She would complain.

This car had flippers as indicators only one of which ever worked so her sudden, left turns were the stuff of nightmares.

Gin and Dubonnet might have also played their part in this unpredictable navigation.

I was prepped for my test by an oldish, almost permanently drunk, retired Irish cavalry officer who had fallen on hard times and made ends meet by driving a tractor and, on terrifying occasions, a horsebox for a local farmer. His driving was even more eccentric than my parents' and he tried never to use the clutch, ramming the gearstick into place, making terrible grinding noises while he muttered darkly 'Come on you little fucker.'

My three tutors had barely any idea between them what any of the road signs meant and, unless they had a number attached to them, 30 MPH say, or an instruction in plain and obvious English like STOP! they disregarded them. Even ones that allowed no room for misinterpretation were met with their own highly personal conclusions.

At that stage I had never driven in a town and I doubt that I had met more than fifty other cars in my whole driving career along the North Riding's sparsely populated lanes.

I have never been as one with machines and engines and, though I can appreciate the beauty of a brass steam engine or an early Lagonda, throbbing engines, gadgets and low-slung orange vehicles do nothing for me. Expensive cars, boats and planes are something I have never coveted, which is just as well.

Despite my lack of practice, strange tutors and complete ignorance of the highway code, I was quietly confident of passing my test. I assumed that, as so many other people had sailed through, there must be little to it.

You merely had to look at how many cars there were on the roads to believe this.

I arrived at the appointed place rather early and, as I found myself outside a pub, I thought I would have a sandwich and a drink to prepare for the test and steady my nerves.

The examiner arrived in a type of car I had never seen before. I was somewhat thrown by this as it bore no resemblance to either my mother's car, which was what I was most used to, or the cavalryman's old Riley.

It was also red, a rare and *outré* colour in those days.

He got out and bustled round to the other side of the car and joined me on the pavement. I was momentarily confused, forgetting that I wasn't the passenger. He shook my hand and immediately said.

'Have you been drinking?'

I was slightly taken aback.

'I've just had my lunch.' I answered ambiguously.

This question unsettled me, so I wasn't at my most confident or relaxed as I went around to the driver's side and got in. I made myself comfortable and then the examiner, a weaselly-looking man in a lambskin coat, asked me to pull out and continue down the high street. There were many more knobs and dials on his dashboard than I was used to and I must say in my own defence that wondering what they were did interfere with my concentration.

Having looked in my mirror, I indicated, peered over my shoulder and did all the other things I remembered from my eccentric tutorials, so I was fairly confident of my start.

Then he coughed loudly and said,

'You can speed up, if you like.'

At this, I noticed that pedestrians on the pavement were keeping up with us with some ease, so I put my foot on the accelerator and we shot forward as this car's pedal was much more reactive than the soggy ones on my more familiar cars.

So, I found out next, were its brakes as, when I first gently applied them, we stopped very suddenly and the car stalled. I turned the key and we shot forward again. I was just thinking to myself that this really wasn't a very good car when he suddenly asked,

'What is this sign here?'

I hadn't been expecting any questions.

'Well I should think it means no left turn, why, what do you think it means?' I replied.

'No, I'm testing you on the Highway Code.' He said, rather peevishly.

'Why?' I asked.

'Because it is part of the Driving Test.'

He now seemed to be getting distinctly angry, squirming a little in his seat, crossing and uncrossing his legs.

This was a new development as neither my mother nor the galloping Major had mentioned academic questions being part of the test and I must have missed this entirely on the endless forms I had been made to fill in.

We were now going at a reasonable pace and I was changing gear with ever less noise and everything seemed to be going much more smoothly.

I felt I had mastered the accelerator and the brakes as there was now very little lurching and we only stalled once more.

I made up intelligent answers to the signposts and his other 'what do you do if' questions with a mixture of common sense and guess work and thought I was doing pretty well when he pointed at a triangular sign with an exclamation mark in the middle of it.

'What is that?' He asked.

'It's an exclamation mark.' I said.

'I know that, Sir, but what does it mean?'

'It comes at the end of a sentence which has a shout or warning or, I presume, an exclamation in it.' I said, not finding it easy to answer this grammatical question, keep my eyes on the road and work all the knobs and peddles at the same time.

'Yes, Sir, it is indeed a warning,' he said quietly, 'and it is a warning of that which is below it.'

This was a poorly constructed sentence and held little meaning until I realised he meant there had been a second part to the sign. I asked,

'Should we go back and have a look?'

'No, Sir, just keep going.' It was becoming ever more obvious that he didn't like me or my driving and was ever more irritated by the way I was outmanoeuvring him on the answers to the traffic signs.

By now, we had turned back into the town's main street when he suddenly said.

'Turn right here, please?'

I had been concentrating on the next signpost, which had a 30 painted in a red circle, which I knew meant a 30 mph speed limit. I had been looking forward to besting him again so hadn't expected this sudden command. I overreacted a little and, as we turned left, I just clipped the very end of a parked car.

It was genuinely the merest graze, literally brushing the edge of its rear light, but you would have thought we'd had a major collision.

'Stop, stop.' He shrieked, 'You hit that car.'

'It's not yours, is it?' I said by way of a small quip; he was now getting very excited, even hysterical.

'No, it's not.' He said.

I smiled at him to show it was just a joke.

'Well that's alright then.' I added to lower the tension a little but then he screamed, genuinely screamed,

'Stop the car, stop the car.' And he hit the dashboard with his clipboard in a very unnecessary way and I thought what bad luck I'd had to have got, of all the examiners there must have been, this one. He was patently unsuitable and not made of the stuff needed for his job.

I stopped the car as quickly as I could, as he had commanded, and he slid down his seat which skewed his glasses a little. This, frankly, did look comical, so I may have let out a small laugh.

He obviously had no sense of humour at all, so it came as little surprise when he failed me; mainly, it seemed to me, because of an unfortunate clash of personalities.

After this setback, which was a blow to my pride I admit, I never found the time to take my test again and so, with L plates and brave passengers, I drove a succession of my own and other people's cars for ten years or so before Louise discovered that my licence was only a provisional one and banned me from ever driving again.

However, on occasion, I have found myself in situations where it was impossible not to drive as I would have been stranded, missed vital meetings, possibly been kidnapped or even been very late for dinner.

11

THE TUMBLE INN

One of my introductions to grown-up life took place at a hostelry called The Tumble Inn.

In the very early 1960s, just before I became a teenager, my father was stationed in France.

We were living in a pretty, small village a few miles from Fontainebleau and had taken over the beautiful local *manoir*, set in its own walled gardens. It had been turned down as his billet by the American general in charge of NATO as he preferred to have an apartment in the town. His loss was our gain.

Paris was not far away, near enough for a day trip of which we made many, but too distant for just a night out. Nearer to home was The Tumble Inn.

This was a great favourite of my father's. He occasionally took my mother, less so my much older twin sisters and sometimes all of us together but, when everyone else was away and he was in sole charge of me, we would go together and I was allowed much more time downstairs with the grownups before going upstairs.

The inn was like a rather exotic pension with restaurant tables around a small dance floor with a pianist accompanying a very French torch singer in the Piaf mould.

The waiters behaved as French waiters have forever and the waitresses were great fun and always made much of me as, to my knowledge, I was the only person under eighteen ever allowed in.

There were also other young ladies, beautifully turned out in the vampish, Gallic look of the day with nipped in waists and tubular skirts, a look I still love. I seem also to remember pill-box hats, but this might well be an over-fertile imagination. These ladies might join any lady-less tables or even make up numbers at a mixed table if asked.

Thinking back, and conversations since have borne this out, it was a very louche place, not that I had any idea then. It was very French and *laissez-faire* and, despite only being eleven, no-one seemed to be at all put out by my being there.

The whole enterprise was run by the astonishing figure of Lulu.

I had certainly never seen such a colourful creature and even my Aunt Betty in full fig and slap came nowhere near Lulu for sheer visual impact.

I was allowed to stay downstairs for a while and have a Coca Cola and pastries, an unimaginable luxury to a young boy then, while Lulu sat me on her ample lap and stroked my hair, almost white in those days and not far off her own colour.

I would be dressed in striped, flannel pyjamas and a dressing gown made of thick wool in a pattern something like a tartan with a matching cord and piping. I had large, hairy slippers but I don't remember feeling out of place, even though all the men wore dinner jackets and the women what were called cocktail dresses.

She would also make much of me and I revelled in being spoilt by her and the waitresses. This, though, was nothing besides the absolute bliss of being upstairs.

When it was time for me to leave the dining room, Lulu would entrust me to one of her girls, I would kiss everyone goodnight and with a farewell

'Sleep well, sprog, be good.' From my father, I would be taken up to a bedroom.

This room was used by all the girls who worked there to leave their coats, thrown over the huge bed, and to tidy themselves up, gossip and fix their makeup.

I would slip under the giant eiderdown which was suffused with the headiest and most exotic scents imaginable, mixing with the heavy smell of powder and make-up. These fabulous creatures, and they did appear to me to be from another world, would chat to each other in French amongst much ribald laughter. I watched, entranced, as they powdered their noses, redid their lipstick, fluffed up their hair and, sometimes, even straightened the suspenders at the top of their stockings.

When they caught me watching, they would wink and then laugh and I would smile a smile so wide that I thought my face might split in two.

These evenings left a deep impression on me.

As I lay there, one might ruffle my hair or give me a little peck and mutter endearments, again in French. I had no idea what they were saying and no understanding of why I enjoyed it all so much.

It was such a delight that I fought against sleep to savour as much of it as I could and, to this day, I can remember these smells and the chatter, their sense of camaraderie and the luxurious comfort of being there with them.

It was also the first place I ever saw a tartan dinner jacket. It was worn with a parallel-bow tie by an American who sported a crew cut in the manner of the popular crooners of the day.

My father pointed at this man's clothes and said, very gravely,

'I'd rather you ran through the streets of Paris naked, painted orange than you ever wore one of those and, if I see you wearing such a thing, I shall call the police immediately, son or no son.'

I was used to my father's hyperbole, so relished this sort of warning.

One evening, Lulu was busy with some other punters so, instead of being on her knee, I sat next to my father on the banquette behind his table. He suddenly jogged my arm and nodded towards a man further along our banquette at the next table who was obviously very drunk and from whom one of the girls was trying to extricate herself.

I had never witnessed any trouble there but, always lurking, were two huge men standing, arms crossed, at the door who habitually saluted my father and who, I presume, took care of any potential fracas.

The girl gently pulled herself away from the drunk and went back to the bar, leaving him beaming first at us and then expansively around the room.

He gulped his champagne and then made a mess of refilling his coupe from the bottle lodged in the ice bucket on his table. Each time he picked up the bottle one of the waitresses tried to help, but was always just too late to stop him spilling most of it onto the table so, after a few attempts, they gave up.

Finally, the bottle was empty which confused him.

He tried first to pour from the empty bottle and, when nothing came out, held it upside down and then peered into it. A last, stray drop or two of champagne must have escaped and dripped into his eye because he yelped and dropped the bottle, which broke his glass as it fell, then rolled off the table onto the floor.

The noise attracted a few stares but did not move the man on the table next to him, two away from us, ensconced as he was with another of the girls.

The boozer put his finger to his lips, 'Shhhh.' He hissed at the bottle and then caught our eyes, which were fixed on his performance, winked at us and pointed to the floor and then shuffled himself down, below his tablecloth in search of the bottle. He reappeared, triumphantly, like a magician, with the bottle just as a waitress arrived at his table, swept the broken glass into a little dustpan and took away the empty.

She returned a few moments later with a new bottle and glass. As she opened it, he patted the seat next to him and motioned to the champagne. The waitress poured some into his new glass and, as he made to touch her wrist, she caught hold of his hand and tweaked his nose while he remained inert and silent but still beaming with impish goodwill.

My father turned back to face our table and I sensed, as he did, that if we were caught watching him again, the drunk would play up to us, depriving us of a genuine performance.

Our friend began to look around restlessly for something to do.

His eyes finally settled on the man to his left along the banquette whose back was facing him as he was turned to his side in deep conversation with the hostess at his table.

The angle at which he was sitting caused his jacket pocket to fall open.

With a look of devilish cunning, the drunk picked a sugar lump from the bowl on his table and dropped it into his neighbour's open pocket. Then he put his hand over his mouth to stifle a giggle.

He repeated this, incredibly slowly and carefully, chuckling after each lump, while my father and I watched with mounting delight. Finally, he had emptied the entire bowl without his victim noticing.

This had taken some time and, as a reward to himself, he drank an astonishing amount of champagne very quickly and, with each gulp, he reacted as if he had swallowed a lemon, pursing his lips and shaking his shoulders and head.

The empty bowl was a problem and he began to look elsewhere on his table for more ammunition and, when he started to weigh up the sugar bowl itself, we held out little hope of his not being rumbled.

We looked at each other and shook our heads; it was never going to fit, especially with the sugar lumps already in there. As he held it in his hand and peered into the open pocket, we could almost hear his brain making calculations.

Then he looked around to see if he was being watched as, even in his cups, he must have realised the bowl was a do-or-die manoeuvre.

He noticed us watching him and raised a quizzical brow. We both shook our heads at him and gave him the thumbs down, but a huge smile spread across his face.

He turned back and tried to slip the bowl gently into the man's pocket but, almost immediately, it met resistance. Undeterred, he pushed it down hard until it forced its way through the pocket opening and down amongst the sugar lumps.

This sudden, violent tug at his pocket alerted the man who turned around quickly enough to catch the perpetrator turning away to adopt the classic innocent's face, eyes rolling to heaven and lips set in a soundless whistle.

The moment the victim put his hand into his pocket he found the mystifying content. He tried to extricate it but found even more resistance trying to dislodge it than our friend had encountered inserting it.

It soon became obvious that he was a Frenchman and the inebriate was an Irishman.

They stereotyped their two great cultures. The Irishman hooted with laughter and slapped his thighs while the Frenchman became outraged by his behaviour. Even though he wasn't yet quite sure what had been done to him, he sensed that he'd been, in some way, made to look a fool in front of his coquette.

He performed a huge, Gallic shrug as he pointed at the bulge in his pocket. The Irishman pointed at the sugar bowl on the Frenchman's table and then at the bulge. This, obviously, made no sense to the Frenchman as it was illogical.

He shrugged again which drew an even bigger hoot from the Irishman who then tried to offer him champagne from his bottle.

The Frenchman looked as if he might be placated but, when he held out his glass to be filled, the Irishman moved the bottle slightly to one side and poured a long, frothing jet of its contents into his lap.

This was too much for the Frenchman and he rose to his feet, wiped the champagne from his trousers and looked down at the Irishman whose straightening face showed that he realised he might have gone too far.

This was certainly our opinion and loyalties vacillated as we waited for the next move.

He slowly picked up the sugar bowl from his table and might well have brought it down on the Irishman's head had his girl not stayed his hand and the drunk not made a run for it while his grin, which had disappeared when things had become ugly, returned to his face.

He ran straight for the bar where Lulu was propped up on a stool chatting to some customers. He was obviously well known and well-liked by her as she smiled and winked hugely at him as he came, in a sort of fast, low lurch, towards her.

The Frenchman, feeling suddenly impotent after the Irishman's departure, and still with the bowl in his hand, did the first aggressive thing that came into his mind and threw it at him.

His throw was not the throw of a cricketer, fast and flat, but of a *bouliste*, so it looped rather lethargically to where its target had been a moment earlier, landed on a table making a terrible noise and causing no little breakage. Then it bounced, throwing sugar lumps everywhere, landed on the floor with a clang and rolled past Loulou to rest at the feet of one of her Neanderthal bouncers.

My father shot me a delighted and enthralled look, wide-eyed at all the possibilities.

In a London nightclub of this sort in those days, a somewhat drunk man with a young, professional lady in tow, would almost be expected to throw a sugar bowl at some stage but, in a place that very much prided itself on its sophistication, this was an outrage, especially coming from a native.

His lady companion had fled from the table when the sugar bowl was lobbed, so he now stood alone, his hand still raised in the classic *boule* follow through position, a picture of guilt.

He was obviously not a regular and, as the bouncer picked up the bowl, he glanced at Lulu who nodded towards the thrower and flicked her head towards the door.

The two huge men approached the Frenchman and shuffled him towards the exit as he tried to explain himself. One of the giants put his finger to his lips and he fell silent. As he reached Lulu he attempted to explain his action but was met with cold contempt.

A waitress brought over his bill on a tray as he stood in silence, just feet away from the gurning, triumphant Irishman, once more slapping his thigh in delight.

As the Frenchman looked at the bill a skein of outrage slid over his face and he was about to argue when one of the bouncers again put finger to lip.

He pulled out his wallet and began to deal notes onto the salver. Then, as he was putting it back, Loulou snapped her fingers at him and said,

'*Et pour Mademoiselle?*'

He took out a few more notes. '*Et pour le sucre?*'

He threw down another note with an angry flourish and the boys escorted him out of the front door.

Pa looked around the room, smiled very contentedly and said, 'Marvellous.'

He looked over at the Irishman and said,

'Splendid.'

It was as good an introduction to grown-up behaviour as you could hope for.

Years later, possibly in my forties, I was talking to my mother about The Tumble Inn. I couldn't remember us ever having discussed it and I was intrigued to hear her take on the place and so I mentioned how affectionate Lulu had always been.

'She was always so kind to me.' I said.

'He, you mean.' My mother corrected.

'Sorry?' I stared at her. 'Sorry, what do you mean?'

'Lulu was a chap.' She said. 'A man.'

I looked at her, incredulously.

'Lulu was a chap; he was a transvestite. You know, he dressed up in girl's clothes.'

'Really?' I said.

I was poleaxed, not so much by this revelation, which in retrospect was obvious, but by my mother's display of urbanity and insouciance, attributes I had never credited her with.

12

BACKING INTO THE LIMELIGHT

In 1981 I was in Los Angeles, meandering up Sunset Boulevard, when to my astonishment I saw the image of two friends of mine reproduced on a billboard as high as a skyscraper.

I slowed to peer up at this mirage through the windscreen – causing much hooting from the cars behind – and realised it was an advertisement for a film that both these two actors had told me was to be no more than a low-budget Indie film.

It was called *Chariots of Fire*, hadn't yet been released in Britain but had taken America by storm.

I had known Nigel Havers since we were young. He'd had great success on television and was making a name for himself as a romantic lead. He was hilarious, self-effacing, great fun and a very good actor.

The other actor was Ben Cross who was also hilarious company, funny and talented but more complicated.

He died much too young but there was always something about him that suggested he mightn't make old bones.

His forte was the angst-ridden outsider both on and off the screen.

These two had been perfectly cast in the film, Nigel as the exquisite dilettante and hurdling aristocrat and Ben, as the angry, quasi-professional, win-at-all-costs sprinter.

Ben, though prone to sink for periods into a dark fog of anger or depression was, when his head was above these clouds, uproarious company and a gifted, spontaneous singer and giver of improvised turns. Almost my favourite kind of complicated friend!

He could keep whole pubs, restaurants or parties amused for hours with his schtick. Sometimes this could go too far. His reading of a crowd could be poor to say the least, but this also added to the danger he relished so much and made his company such an exciting proposition.

I remember an *ad hoc* set of 'Adolph Dylan' songs he invented on the spot and sang wearing a small moustache which failed spectacularly to amuse an open-mouthed audience in a Bierkeller.

Chariots of Fire gave both of them the sort of instant stardom which Nigel took with the pinch of salt befitting an Englishman but Ben, who was out in LA at the time, jumped into with both feet and relished every moment.

It was extraordinary to walk down the street or go into a restaurant with him - and extremely irritating - to find him called out, feted and flirted with by women of every age and provenance.

Ben had recently played the lead in *Chicago the Musical*, in London which had given him the chance to act, dance, sing in his loud and true voice and generally show off.

But *Chariots of Fire* completely changed his life and made him a rising star, teetering on the verge of real stardom. What he did with this opportunity is a cautionary tale for all young actors, but I am assuming anyone reading this is too old for cautionary tales to make any difference so I'll spare the lecture.

So it was that, at the height of his new popularity in Hollywood, Ben and I, along with a few friends and locals, walked into *La Cage aux Folles* cabaret club in LA.

This establishment was loosely based on the club in the superlative French comedy of that name and had the viperish but adorable Gypsy at front of house who also acted as the MC.

Her Drag Queen persona was one of her own invention, but the other cabaret acts, except the chorus, all dressed up as and brilliantly imitated real stars, dead or alive, miming to their best known numbers.

The drag Tina Turner impersonator, for instance, might sing 'River Deep Mountain High' and not just look and gyrate like her but mime so closely it was hard to believe it wasn't the great diva herself on stage. So Dolly Parton, Bette Midler, Diana Ross would appear and then a superb Judy Garland who, during the act, metamorphosed superbly into her daughter, Liza Minelli.

When Marilyn Monroe came over to thank Ben for the drink he had sent her, she flirted outrageously and stole the hearts of everyone at our table.

Part restaurant, part club and part theatre, it housed a strange cocktail of an audience.

There were coachloads of out-of-towners, who had come to be slightly and enjoyably shocked and dip their toes into the wild side; they were noisy and delighted by everything and mainly sat at the back.

Next was a stratum of the city's well-off residents who all understood the references and felt they were having an edgy night. Finally, at the front were the best-heeled diners at the very expensive tables. These were mainly showbiz, some rich gays at their dazzling, mixed tables, all exquisitely dressed and coiffed, and then some rich young revellers and a smattering of LA's ubiquitous and fabulously turned-out old starlets and fag-hags.

There were also a few tables of utterly bemused people who had obviously not read the small print.

At the end of each act, Gypsy sashayed onto the stage and, blinking into the spotlight, thanked everyone for being there, dropped double-entendres like confetti and insulted one or two of her friends in the audience whose proclivities were obviously well known to the more worldly of the crowd.

Then, towards the end of one of her spiels, she suddenly said.

'Well, ladies and gentlemen...and not so gentle men...... and those are my kinda men...'

You have probably gathered the tone of the evening by now....

'We have someone in the audience tonight,' and you could hear the inflexion that made it sound as if it should be spelled tonite,

'......we have someone in the audience that is going to blow your little bobby socks off. He's a huge talent, he's just starred in the most fabulous movie that we all loved – and if you haven't seen it get out there now...no, actually, wait until you've paid your bill and tipped the girls..

So, folks of all sizes and heights put your hands together and give a big, Hollywood welcome to the star of *Chariots of Fire* Mr Ben Cross.'

A spotlight slipped its beam over onto Ben and he rose to his feet trying to look modest, not his natural look.

We were right at the front and our table was almost on top of the slightly raised stage so Gypsy put out her hand to pull Ben up. He stood, grinning by her side, and held up his palms to acknowledge the thunderous applause from the crowd. It didn't abate until Gypsy motioned to him to grab the other microphone and said,

'Ben, this is such an honour, I am about to faint.' Ben grinned.

'I feel the same way, Gypsy.' He joshed.

'Now Ben, you've just been the lead in *Chicago* in the West End of London, and they tell me you have terrific pipes.'

The audience was beginning to see where this was going and had started a persuasive, slow clap.

'Whadya think, kids?' Gypsy continued 'Do we want a number from Ben?'

Ben smiled and put his hand up to quell the noise.

'I have a better idea.' He said and looked conspiratorially out at the audience.

'I have, right here at my table, the man who is currently taking London by storm and who will soon be opening on Broadway.'

Like everyone else I looked around our table. There were only the two locals that I didn't know and neither looked like a leading man or even a singer, but you never knew.

As we were all giving each other sidelong glances Ben continued.

'He's been called the heir to Elvis and the second Sinatra.' He paused.

'Do you want to hear him?' he shouted and, as they all screamed 'Yeeeeessss' back at him, he stamped his foot and bellowed,

'I said ...DO YOU WANT TO HEAR HIM?' and then he pointed at me. A different spotlight shone into my face and Gypsy went nuts.

I was bundled onto the stage by laughing 'friends' and found myself blinking into the lights while the crowd went absolutely wild.

Gypsy kissed me hello. Ben handed me the microphone, shushed the crowd and stepped quickly off the stage, leaving me alone in the harsh spotlight apart from a wry old pianist, sitting quietly and looking at me expectantly, gently shaking his head at human folly.

I was in turmoil and caught between a strangely convincing fantasy that I would open my mouth and, magically, a fabulous voice would emanate and bring the house down - a moment that would become the opening scene of the 'Theo Legend' - and the awful truth that I had been landed in it by Ben with absolutely nowhere to go but headlong into a deep pit of humiliation.

I decided to throw myself on the mercy of the crowd. 'I'm so sorry,' I started 'but my voice is shot, jet lag, you know....'

Why in God's name didn't I just tell them it was all just Ben's silly joke?

I suspect it was because I was rather enjoying myself, being on stage in Hollywood, and didn't want it to end immediately. I realised this was misbegotten thinking, only just not quickly enough, so I tried to make a joke of it.

However, the crowd had other thoughts.

'Sing, sing.....' they shouted and my table also began to shout and bang the table so that a rhythmic and primal chant of 'sing, sing, sing..' began to rumble through the club.

My friends were making things worse by setting up a counter shout of 'Thee-oh-oh' and so, standing in front of this maelstrom, I suddenly decided to go for it.

I put up my hand to silence my fans and looked over at the pianist.

The crowd, sensing something memorable was about to happen, went quiet.

'Which number can I play for you?' asked the pianist.

'Sorry?' I replied.

'Which song would you like me to play?' I could see his suspicions were raised.

'Ah, yes, ummm.' I mused.

I realised this was all taking too long, 'These Foolish Things?'

'OK, great. Key?' 'Sorry?'

'What key?' he saw my blank face. 'What key would you like me to play it in?'

'Ah, yes, well, what key do you like?' I asked back.

'Shall we go for C?' He suggested.

'Good choice.' I replied. 'I love C.'

'Sung intro or straight into the song?' He continued.

This was getting tedious for the audience and my nerve was failing fast. Adrenal courage doesn't last long, and I could sense the crowd was turning.

'Straight in.' I replied confidently.

He then tickled the ivories. There are genuinely no other words to describe what he did.

Decades of accompanying crooners and bar singers all over the States had given him a lightness of touch that was sublime. I was so struck by his skill that I forgot to come in on time, so he tinkled on to give me a second stab.

'*A cigarette that bears a lipstick's traces,*' I began, and it was immediately obvious to almost everybody that this was not the voice that was conquering the West End.

'*An airline ticket to romantic places.*' I continued and then the murmuring began at the back of the club.

Out of the corner of my eye I could see Ben, and many others, kneeling in cruel but supressed laughter. Some people at my table were actually crying with mirth.

'*Oh, how the ghost of you clings, these foolish things remind me of you.*'

A little ripple from the pianist and then,

'*Da dee dee dum dum dee dee dum....*' I couldn't remember a single other foolish thing.

I had sung and listened to this song a thousand times and knew the words, I thought, by heart.

'I'm so sorry.' I stopped singing but the pianist continued. In fact, he 'took it away' and extemporised loudly as I was trying to explain that it was all a misunderstanding.

A complete shambles was averted by Gypsy realizing what the crowd hadn't, that this was a childish wheeze by Ben.

There was proper booing, I mean people actually articulating the word boo, and it was very loud.

I had been catcalled before, had various missiles thrown at me and faced silence from disappointed punters, but I had never been booed, certainly not as roundly as this.

I think I was hissed as well.

I slunk down off the stage.

Meanwhile, Ben had made his way up and over to the pianist and, after a very brief chat, launched into a fantastically professional version of *The Lady is a Tramp* and, before the wild applause had died, he was into a heart- breaking rendition of *Night and Day*. When the clapping settled to just loud, he motioned me up to the stage but, before I even moved a muscle, people started to boo again so Ben, wisely, sent me back and leapt into his finale, *You'll Never Walk Alone.*

As he finished the place went mad and Gypsy came on to congratulate him and lead a standing ovation.

It was time for the grand finale.

All the acts came out for a medley of their 'own' songs and Marilyn did *I Want to be Loved by You* in such a sexy way that we thought one of the men with us might pass out.

When it was all over, we stayed at our table while the audience and diners left. I was sitting next to Ben and everyone wanted to shake his hand.

As they came over, they combined their fawning over Ben with poisonous looks at me. Showbiz is no laughing matter in L.A.

It was so unnerving that I asked Ben to explain to them that I wasn't really in showbiz and that it had all been a joke.

I couldn't hear what he was saying to these besotted fans but the looks became increasingly threatening and disgusted as the final members of the audience left, so I rather doubt he had followed my instructions.

We were soon the only people left in the club and Gypsy joined us along with most of the performers now mostly back in their own clothes, some still in drag but others in unexpectedly prosaic male outfits.

At least I had a chance to apologise to Gypsy and then the pianist and to explain that it had all been a joke on Ben's part.

The ivory tinkler leant over to me and in a world-weary voice said,

'Don't worry. I've played for much bigger assholes than you.'

I laughed but, on reflection, it seemed to infer that I didn't even make it as an asshole.

13

HIGH SOCIETY

Back in the early 1980s, I had made friends with Paul, an American I'd met at Doctor Zack's place in LA.

Paul's suave, preppy looks and elegant manners belied a very surprising person. Enigmatic might be the best word to describe him.

When we met again, back in London, he was living in an opulent penthouse in Eaton Square and walking out with a famously beautiful and spoilt Euro-Royal. Everything suggested a playboy with a rich, WASP background. I found out later that he was actually flat-sitting for some vague friends and had only met this lady a couple of days before and that she knew as little about him as I did.

That evening we ended up in Tramp where he introduced me to a bold new drinking concept. This was called 'Top Shelf' There was no great complexity to it. It only needed one of those huge brandy balloons that most bars have on display as a novelty and a nimble barman to hop up to the top shelf and then pour out a shot from each dusty bottle displayed there. These were the liquors that no-one ever ordered and there was a good reason for that.

Drunk separately they were hideous enough but, mixed together, it required both great courage and having no plans for the next few days.

We refined this drink into an even riskier version where the contents were randomly chosen but I can no longer remember how. This was called 'The Trash Can'.

One of Paul's many attributes was to live life as an adventure. He had a tendency to disappear, sometimes for long periods, only to re-emerge in your life in a different place with a completely random job, support mechanism and set of plans. But movies were and remained his great love and no one suited that world better.

We were both in our early thirties, I would guess, when he rang to ask if I would bring a cricket team out to Rhode Island and stay with him at Beechwood, the Astors' legendary *fin de siècle*, cliff-top house, which he assured me was now his. This sounded unlikely, but good fun, and apparently there was room for everyone to stay there with him. I worked out that Louise and I could combine it with a trip to NY for a very important meeting..

Paul's new house had been chosen as the venue for that year's English Speaking Union Ball, a high spot of the Newport season, so he told me. The Australian yacht was in harbour for the America's Cup races and he had managed to get a long weekend entirely sponsored by Taittinger and Pimm's. It sounded both good fun and cheap, so I said I would try and put a team together.

He assured me that we just needed to bring the cricket equipment, pay for our plane tickets and he and the sponsors would do the rest.

I eventually managed to assemble a fairly disparate team made up of friends who played cricket reasonably well but none of whom were the sort of toffs that Paul and the sponsors were obviously hoping for.

Without mobile telephones and modern communications, trying to organise this rabble was almost impossible and, at the airport, I had to resort to the PA system on three occasions to try and corral them.

The team with wives and girlfriends made nearly twenty people and, after a very messy, boozy flight and an embarrassing interlude at customs, which reflected well on nobody, we found three big cars waiting for us and so set off for Beechwood, Newport, Rhode Island.

There was some real excitement, on arrival, as none of us had been prepared for the grandness of what had once been the Astors' summer 'cottage'. It was extremely large, grand, in a sort of Versailles-meets-Weybridge way, and imposing. I could feel my stock rising amongst the more cynical of our team.

I rang the doorbell and nothing happened so I tried again and finally heard footsteps clacking across the hall. There was also the unexpected sound of a horse trotting up behind us. I was about to turn around to investigate when the door opened and a pretty Edwardian maid greeted me. She was wearing a long black dress, a bib-fronted white apron and a mobcap. She bobbed us a little curtsy and said.

'Good evening, Sir.' And, as Louise stepped forward, she added. 'and Ma'm. Are you here to see Mrs Astor?'

We stood there in silence, confused. There was a whinny and I turned to find a horse on which a lady in full hunting rig, top hat, veil, and a long skirt, sat side-saddle, beaming a bright Hollywood smile.

'I was going to say that Mrs Astor was out,' continued the maid, 'but here she is now, back from her evening hack.'

I turned round to face Mrs Astor.

'How lovely, I hear you've come to stay.' She said in clipped, Katherine Hepburn tones and rode off to the back of the house.

The maid, obviously as perplexed at our arrival as we were by our reception, disappeared.

Then one of my friends said,

'You didn't tell us Paul was an Astor.'

'Well, I don't think he is.' I replied, 'I'm sure he would have told me, how very strange.'

Eventually a louche, unruffled looking man arrived in a sports car and introduced himself as a friend of Paul's. He didn't appear to know much about any plans either but did know that some of us would be staying at the house and others would be 'on the yacht'.

After a brief but complicated discussion, three couples volunteered to stay on the boat and were driven off to the harbour.

Louise and I were left with a few other couples to stay in the big house. Our suitcases were whisked away by more Edwardian maids and a valet and we were shown into a huge and incredibly tidy kitchen.

As we stood around waiting, a hint of unease crept over us. We sensed that we might be in the wrong house or had perhaps arrived on the wrong day. There was something curious about our situation, as if we were in an episode of 'The Prisoner'.

I noticed a loaf of bread and a knife on the kitchen table, so I went to cut a bit off as I was starving. I put my hand on the loaf to hold it down and recoiled as the bread was as cold as a stone and as hard. This was because it was stone and, when I laid the knife against the loaf, it made no impression other than causing a little chip to fly out of the top of it.

'It's not real.' I said, 'It's fake bread. It's stone. What the fuck?' Our host appeared.

'Theo, Louise, darlings, so good to see you! You made it.' Paul smiled his winning smile which lit us all with its beam.

'We've been waiting for ages. Now where do you want us to go?' said one of my team, rather impolitely, determined not to be charmed.

'Oh, I am so sorry, I had no idea. Why don't I get someone to take you up to your rooms? Theo and Louise, you're in the Astors' room.'

'Wonderful, thanks.' I said and went up close to him and whispered, 'Everyone's starving and bursting for a drink. Is there anything I can get them?'

Paul took me aside to a corner of the kitchen and in a somewhat furtive voice said.

'I may not have made this completely clear but the thing is, Theo,' he paused 'although this is, in many, many ways, my house, it is also kind of a living museum.'

'What the fuck is that?' I asked.

'Well, with a little bit of help from some others, I have done up the house and restored it to how it would have been when the Astors lived here, you understand?'

I nodded but things were still unclear.

'Then people pay to come here and see how it would have been in the golden days. I get out-of-work actors to play the part of the servants and stuff.' He paused to let this sink in.

'They stay in character all the time as well. It's quite tiresome.' He added with a sigh.

'We call it resting.' I said.

'What?' Asked Paul.

'When actors are out of work.' I said.

'Why the fuck does that matter?' He asked.

'Well it's just a euphemism that protects their pride.' I explained

'That makes no sense.' He said out loud, our strange little conversation had, up to then, been held in a hissing whisper.

'You have to have no pride to be an actor in the first place.'

It wasn't the time to start a discussion on the usefulness or otherwise of Thespians but all the Edwardian maids, Mrs Astor and the grooms hanging around the house began to make sense, as did the pristine kitchen.

'I should maybe have mentioned that this is all kinda like a big stage set.' He conceded. 'There is a small private bit where you guys are staying, but the rest is sorta......'

His voice petered out.

'Yes, perhaps you should have.' I said.

I suddenly had a worrying thought. 'There actually is a yacht, isn't there?'

'Of course there is.' He answered, looking hurt.

I was trying to compute what all this might mean when I noticed, for the first time, that Paul was wearing a dinner jacket, so I said,

'Shit, the party isn't tonight, is it?'

No, no,' he reassured me 'I just have to go to a fund-raiser tonight so you can all relax.'

'Are we eating here?' I asked looking around at the spotless kitchen.

'No, no, no, of course not….listen, I gotta go, see you all later. And with an insouciant wave, he was gone.

'I'm so sorry.' I began turning back to face the others. 'Little bit of a cock up. It seems we are sleeping in the private part of the house but the rest of it is a sort of living museum.' I explained, borrowing Paul's phrase.

'I'm afraid there's no food or drink here, I continued 'so we will have to fend for ourselves and make the most of it. The party and the cricket are all here at the house so that's nice and convenient for us so here's only for sleeping and….'

'It is what it is.' One of the wives said philosophically in a very tired voice. 'Can we just get our stuff to our rooms, have a wash and get something to eat.'

We struggled up the stairs with the maids chatting to us in their Edwardian lingo and then the one leading the way stopped outside a huge door and said,

'Mr and Mrs Fennell, you're in here, please be careful of all the decorations and fittings and keep all your possessions out of sight.'

She said this in quite a stern voice but, before I could question her request, she opened the door into a magnificent bedroom, as opulently decorated as it would have been in the Astors' day, unnerving in its stillness.

'This is your bedroom, Sir and Ma'am.' She announced.

'The bathroom is through there.' she said pointing to a large double door.

'If you other ladies and gentlemen could follow me, please.' She said and, throwing us another little curtsy, took the others upstairs.

After a brief wash, we went downstairs to find the others, armed with some plastic mugs and diving into their duty free.

'How are your rooms?' I asked Malcolm, normally the most relaxed and charming of people.

'Room!' He snapped, 'We've only got one fucking room, one shower and a cupboard thing in the wall between all of us. Two of us are sleeping in the fucking cupboard. You said it would be like a five-star hotel..... ....my arse.' He ended, lost for a witty ending to his rant.

'I don't think I said five-star......' I started, but I was cut off by Malcolm saying,

'No, you actually said better than five stars, the lap of luxury, you said, like an Eastern potentate's palace, you said.'

There was an uncomfortable silence.

I might have, when it was looking as if we could be short of a few players, overstated the opulence of where we were to be staying and even exaggerated the quality of the food and drink. I now realised this had been unwise as I'd had no idea at the time and it was fuelling the sceptics who were, it now seemed, a majority.

We were to meet the others at a place called The Arc and, when we gathered downstairs, there was a definite frisson in the air.

I drank my drink alone.

I felt we should move on and asked the maid if she could get us a car.

'I may be able to find a carriage, Sir.' She answered, still in character, and Paul was right, it did get tiresome.

'Look, don't worry about staying in character when you're with us.' I told her. 'We'll take it as read that you're an Edwardian maid and when there's no one around we can all just be normal.'

'I don't know to what you are referring, Sir, but I will make haste and order your carriage.' And off she bustled, resting but not inactive.

The cabs eventually came and took us to The Arc, where we were to have dinner. Those staying on the yacht were as happy as sand-boys and had no sympathy for us, squeezed into the big house, as they assumed we had chosen what we thought would be the better option.

I remained very quiet about Louise and I taking the bedroom that had been the Astors'.

My friend, Zac, was already staying upstairs at The Arc with a very handsome blonde lady who, though not in the very first flush of youth, was exuberant, striking and, it turned out, had no behavioural boundaries whatsoever.

She made it instantly clear that she was a rabid Estonian nationalist and it was her life's ambition to free her country from the Soviet yoke.

'How come you're staying here, Zac?' My question came during a lull in the conversation, so everyone turned to hear his answer.

'Because I've known Paul much longer than you guys.' He said ruefully and then guffawed as he so often did.

Dinner seemed to put everybody in a better mood and we all had an early night.

I awoke in Mr Astor's room to the sunbeams of a beautiful day burning through the windows.

There was an 1890s newspaper on my bedside table so I took it to read on the grand mahogany throne that had been the Astors' loo.

I was engrossed in the report of a murder trial from almost a century before and Louise was naked, putting on her make-up, when there was a strange kerfuffle from the other side of our bathroom door and a distinct murmur of people.

We froze and looked at each other.

'And this is Mr and Mrs Astor's bathroom.' A loud voice said outside.

We realised that we were about to become naked players in a belle epoque soap.

The bathroom had no lock and the doorknob began to rattle. As it was turning, Louise managed to grab it on our side and hold it closed tight. There was a brief wrestle and a wittering of mystified voices.

I snapped out of my reverie on the lavatory, jumped up and pulled the chain. The clang and Niagaran flushing noise of the Edwardian contraption created an instant hush. It was such an incongruous noise, coming from an otherwise silent Museum, that it confused everyone for a moment. The guide, hosting the first tour of the day, was more astonished than anyone as she had no idea that there was anyone staying, but she improvised beautifully.

'Oh, Mr Astor seems to be at home and about his business so, please, let's move on.'

This hiccup in our plans for a leisurely lie-in was followed, almost immediately, by Paul running into our room without knocking, in a panic.

'Fuck's sake, the tours have started and no-one is up yet. You were meant to be out of here by nine.'

'I'm sorry but no-one told us we had to be out by nine or that there were tours or....'

I was cut off by Paul shushing me as he ran out of the room. A moment later he rushed back in.

'OK, so let's get everyone from upstairs out and go get some breakfast.' He said and disappeared again.

I was just putting on my trousers and Louise was using the only functioning - and cold - tap, when there was another brouhaha further down the hall. The same poor tour guide had discovered more sets of sleeping, befuddled guests in the other bedrooms.

Unhappy with their sleeping arrangements, a choice of mattresses on the floor in the attic or squeezed into the cupboard, they had all come down a flight of stairs and taken over three of the other exhibition bedrooms. I had enough clothes on to explore the source of this noise so I went along with Paul to the next room where two of our group were still in bed.

'What the fuck are you doing?' Paul said to the groaning couple and added, oddly, I thought, 'And where did you get those sheets from?'

The two in bed were hungover, jet-lagged and had no idea where they were, let alone that there was a tour of midwestern rubberneckers waiting outside their room to learn how grandees lived in the good old days.

'From the mattresses upstairs.' Said the girl finally and defensively. 'We brought them down with us.'

For some reason this seemed to settle Paul a little but not the waiting group who were trying to stretch their necks around the door hoping this might be living, bedroom theatre.

'So who's upstairs?' his question was answered by someone sticking their head out of the next-door bedroom a few feet down the hall and loudly asking the reasonable question,

'What the fuck is going on?'

I tried to explain what was happening when a second tour took up its station outside our bedroom. I walked back with as much speed and dignity as I could to tell the guide - this one was dressed as a vintage children's nurse - that there was going to be a delay ahead of her and she should probably take the tour another way.

Paul took me aside and said,

'Please, please. Can you get everyone to just clear their rooms and take all their stuff back upstairs. These kids have just opened a cupboard and found three naked people hiding......that's not good.'

Then he continued.

'One had his briefs on his head.'

'Briefs?' I questioned.

'What are briefs?'

'You know, shorts.'

'No, I don't know.' I replied but this was wasting time and Paul was obviously in a hurry.

'Pants.' Said Louise.

'What?' Paul and I said together.

'You know, underpants.' She explained.

'Well why didn't you say so?' I asked Paul.

Paul was now showing severe signs of stress and impatience.

'For fuck's sake, it's not important. Get everyone to take all their things and bedclothes back upstairs now and avoid the tours. Let's get this place back to normal.' Paul said in a raised voice.

'Normal?' I said, laying on the irony, 'Normal?'

A disgruntled gathering reconvened for breakfast back at The Arc.

We were met by the yacht guests with faces so choleric that I thought there must have been murder in the night.

'Anything wrong?' I asked.

'Only that we got turfed off the fucking boat at six this morning because Paul has chartered the fucking thing without telling us.' One of them explained.

'It turns out it's not even his yacht. We'd only just unpacked our clothes and then this fucker comes on board and....'

His hangover took away any further momentum.

'So where are we going to sleep now?' He finished.

It was a good point.

'You told us it was going to be like a five-star....' Another refugee from the yacht began.

'Yes, yes, I know,' I answered.

'Sack the tour leader.' Somebody said and not for the first time.

I noticed Paul was hanging back near the door, so I turned to him.

He shrugged, slipped back behind the lintel and melted away.

The obvious flaws developing in my promised plan of a luxurious and all but free holiday were beginning to dent everyone's faith in me so I decided I should step back up as team leader.

We asked if we could take three double rooms at The Arc for the human flotsam and agreed we would all split the cost.

The six of us staying at Beechwood had weaved our way back after a protracted lunch to change for the party. We had no idea what the point of this ball was, what it entailed and characteristically, Paul had not briefed us.

It seemed it was a feather in his cap, or at least the house's, to host this very smart evening. The Duke of Marlborough, whose soubriquet Sunny was not wholly apt, was giving us all a speech about Blenheim Palace after dinner and Paul told us that this was another feather in his cap, though we doubted it.

He asked us to be on our very best behaviour and be downstairs and ready at six to greet the guests.

Dutifully most of us trotted downstairs on time to be met by a glorious vista.

The ballroom had been transformed throughout in white and gold.

The linen, curtains and flowers all melded into an astonishing indoor snowscape. The tall French windows were open and the bright, emerald lawn, faultlessly mown, slipped away to an abrupt, green horizon beyond which there were only the flawless, turquoise sea and the azure sky.

In the foreground the paved terrace was surrounded by a floral border as bright as any hallucinogenic dream.

All the waiters were dressed in dapper period liveried costumes.

The waitresses in black dresses, white aprons and caps were the stuff of adolescent dreams; or is that just me?

It really was a gorgeous picture; I was genuinely moved and even when Bill slid up to me and said,

'Fucking special, this is.' The period harmony of the scene remained unspoiled.

Sadly, having been so punctual, by the time the first guests began to arrive, our receiving party was noticeably over-refreshed.

These early arrivals appeared to be that type of old, rich American, still full of founding father's blood and a hardy breed. Many continued to go to parties until there was literally no life left in them, drank like fish and still remained all but sober. I have sat next to silent and almost motionless centurions in America who were still determined to have a social life.

Once, at a strange party in LA, I was introduced by my bounder of an Irish host to an old-fashioned blonde bombshell. She was in her mid-twenties and entirely bedecked with diamonds, pushing a wheelchair in which was slumped a man so grey, wrinkled and huddled that it was impossible to guess his age or, for that matter, anything about him. His skin had reached a shiny pallor, pulled so tight on his skull that only the thin, purple slash of his mouth and watery, pale eyes were discernible. Hanging from IV stands screwed to the chair and attached to various parts of his anatomy was a jungle of bottles, bags, spigots and tubes.

When I shook the bombshell's hand, she didn't let go of mine for an uncomfortably long time as she pulled her hair back from her forehead. She was chewing gum in an overtly lascivious way and all conversation had stopped around us.

'This is my hus-bind.' She drawled and waved her hand at the shape in the wheelchair.

I put my hand out to shake his and he didn't move a muscle, but his two rheumy eyes swivelled slowly up to meet mine. There was no recognition, not a blink, and no sign of activity behind them of any sort. I smiled at him and lost for something to say, I asked her,

'Your husband? How nice. Is he enjoying himself?'

She moved her weight from one foot to the other, flicked out her hip, resting on it a hand jangling with bracelets, looked down at him momentarily and then looked me straight in the eyes and, with a sigh of infinite *ennui*, she shrugged and said,

'Who can tell?'

Meanwhile, back at the ball, the guests continued to arrive at Beechwood and our team was getting ever more boisterous. Unfortunately, someone had found the Duke's carousel of slides and mixed up his illustrations of the Palace so that few now matched the order for the lecture.

A delicious dinner finally began but two achingly well-intentioned and very long speeches had been made before we even got as far as the Blenheim talk. This meant that many of the guests, and our tables in particular, had become over-merry and restless.

It so happened that the beam from the slides slightly overlapped the screen throwing a strong shard of light past it, through an open window, and into the blackness beyond. A couple of the women from our group happened to be walking past this window outside and one of them noticed that this horizontal beam struck her upper torso at exactly breast height and spontaneously thought it would be amusing to display hers in this serendipitous spotlight as a sort of flashlight flash.

Having done this, she stepped out of the limelight and disappeared into the darkness as the other girl took her place and so on for a short while. I understand if you think this was childish behaviour, and I would have to agree, but it was a different, less worthy time and it did keep us amused during the turgid speeches.

The locals, not knowing that the breasts belonged to overseas guests, began trying to guess which of their friends had been in the spotlight so that every poor woman coming back into the room from that direction having innocently powdered her nose, was met with a raucous and bawdy cheer. This was a great, somewhat Elizabethan game and lasted until a very old *grande dame* appeared and, after a loud, lone and premature cheer, there was a sudden, embarrassed silence.

The older local grandees all seemed to have a wonderful sense of fun and took genuine delight in this juvenile behaviour.

I noticed, with some alarm, that Bill, my old and raffish friend, had sidled up to a young society journalist and was chatting to her in his inimitable and suggestive style so I hurried over to join them before any damage could be done.

'Ah, Mr Fennell.' She said with one of those bright, expensive, American smiles that always remind me of how shabby my own dentistry is. She was sober, bright as a platinum pin, beautifully turned out, and obviously skilled at dealing with over-familiar interviewees, but Bill was turning on the charm, nonetheless, and seemed put out by my arrival.

'It is Mr Fennell?' She asked.

'Do call me Theo.' I said, eliciting raised eyebrows and a comic leer from Bill who only deals in *double-entendre* and often *pas d'entendre*.

I fashioned a 'don't be ridiculous you're wasting your time here, she's a journalist' sort of shake of the head and shrug for good measure but it was lost on Bill.

'Maybe you can tell me...' and she tested the water with 'Theo?'

'Tell you what?' I asked and Bill made even this innocent question seem salacious.

'The team that you brought out here,' she started, 'does it contain any aristocrats?'

She pronounced the word in the uniquely American way which always makes me think of that great joke.

I now understood Paul's disappointment in the team I had gathered so, as I didn't want to let her down, I hummed for a while to make it appear I was having to think about it,

'I'm not really sure we have, no.'

'Oh my,' she said beaming, 'that is so cool; not even knowing if you have any Lords and Ladies among you.'

I was only too aware that we had little approaching a nob in the team and was thinking how to soften the blow when Bill, sniffing an opening, piped up from behind her.

'Well, there is me, of course.' He was a good-looking man and, annoyingly attractive to women. He used his husky voice brilliantly here in a funny and rustic, but infuriatingly successful, way to seduce; but he was not nobility in any of its forms.

'You, Bill?' She said, turning smartly around to face him. I rolled my eyes at him but his blood was up.

'You, Bill?' I also said.

'Yes, me.' He said with a woeful attempt at aristocratic insouciance.

'I am actually Lord Wiggins.' He pronounced modestly. 'Though I rarely use my title. Actually, Lord Wiggins of Rump.' He added needlessly but I saw where this was going.

'Perhaps you have heard of my country estate, Farkham Hall?' He continued.

It was indeed going exactly where I thought it was.

He had obviously set himself the challenge of seeing how far he could take this before being rumbled. I could have put him out of his misery by telling him that, however broad and suggestive he became, she would take anything he said at face value if she thought there was even the vaguest chance that he was a real English Lord.

'Oh, wait a minute.' She said, 'I just need to take this down.' And, as she scrabbled in her little clutch, Bill added for good measure,

'Take down whatever you like.'

'Really, Bill?' I thought.

She started to write down his address while Bill squeezed out the maximum suggestiveness from each syllable.

'And that's in The Nether Regions.' He added.

Not a flicker crossed her face as she faithfully wrote this all down. Then she looked at Bill and said,

'So, let me see if I have this right. Lord Wiggins of Rump, Farkham Hall in the Nether Regions, England.'

Not a glimmer, Bill nodded and, her job done, she turned around to me and said.

'Thank you so much, kind Sir,' and, with a little bob to Bill, she added, 'and you, my Lord.'

And off she went in search of more blue blood.

I looked at Bill.

He was very pleased with himself.

Years later Bill had finished an affair with a very famous and beautiful actress and was asked by a Sunday newspaper to tell his life story, leaving nothing out. He was offered a great deal of money 'to spill the beans about his whole life' and, being more than usually broke at the time, there was some consternation amongst his friends that he might actually take the money.

When I asked him who would make any sort of appearance in his memoirs, he replied.

'Well, you might but don't worry, I'm changing everyone's name to protect the innocent.' He paused and then shot me a sly look.

'For instance, you're going to be Leo Ferrell, Chelsea Jeweller.' He beamed, tapped the side of his nose and then winked at me.

'See what I mean?' He said, 'Clever.'

Mercifully Bill was extremely decent to all concerned and this opus never saw the light of day.

The Beechwood Ball was shaping up to be a very late night but we knew we had the big cricket match the next day and owed it to our sponsors to put up a good show against the Australians, so we were all in bed by five.

These wild colonial boys were the crew of their country's America's Cup yacht *Australia II*, later that month to make history by winning the cup, the first team ever to wrest it from the Americans since its inception 132 years before.

We suspected that they would be fitter than us.

It had been a brilliant party and so breakfast the next morning was mainly a silent affair. I was quietly reading a local newspaper and turned to the back page where I found a gossip column and a report of the previous evening. There, beside pictures of happy revellers, was an image of Bill, captioned with his bogus title and address in print, verbatim.

The sun was shining and it was going to be a wonderful day.

A cricket square had been beautifully mown and rolled on the huge lawn but, large though this was, its boundaries still made for a very small cricket pitch. One boundary was the steps leading up to the terrace around the house and another was the edge of the cliff that fell away straight down to the beach and the sea. The others were very short and the wicket, though prepared by the lawn tennis groundsman, was no less bumpy than a lawn could be.

In the event, nineteen men and three women, mostly dressed in white, gathered to be photographed and interviewed in this elegant setting. We had brought stumps and pads and all the other cricketing paraphernalia we could manage, so the scene differed little from a village cricket match. There was a small crowd mainly made up of local Americans, some of whom had been at the party the night before and were still suffering.

Whilst we were royally fed and watered by our long-suffering sponsors I tried to clarify, as simply as possible for the local spectators, the rules of the great game. Much has been written about the complexity of trying to explain cricket, especially to Americans for some reason, but a short afternoon game is not that different from baseball. It is just natural impatience that makes a five-day game - with breaks for lunch and tea - seem unimaginable to them.

Amongst our final team were Zac and the Estonian lady who were subs for two people still sleeping off their lunch and two new Englishmen who had come to watch but had never really played the game. We were a motley crew.

The Australian team however, though lacking much in the way of cricketing expertise, was as bursting with muscle and rude health as eleven professional racing yachtsmen have to be.

They won the toss and elected to bat.

The Australian opening batsmen walked out dressed in very white shorts and muscled their way to the square. Someone who had never even seen a game of cricket agreed to umpire and I tried to set a field but no one took any notice of me.

What happened next was unfortunate.

Our brave lad bowled the first ball, and not a bad one. The Australian opener with a mindless heave hit the ball over the cliff and into that land from which no traveller returns. There were hoots from the Australian team and a brash display from the batsman and a new ball was called for.

Unlike baseball, tennis and other, lesser games the cricket ball and its ongoing, deteriorating state is of vital importance to the ebb and flow of a cricket contest, and, in those days, a new ball was a sacred object and, sadly, we had only brought the one, which was now in the sea.

We were either going to have to stop the game, having travelled thousands of miles, or find an alternative.

The only option was a tennis ball, so we extended the teams to all-comers and played sixteen-a-side with people of all ages, ethnicity and sexes joining in.

It was probably the first truly inclusive game of cricket ever played.

Of course, it was not proper cricket as such and so my lack of both runs and wickets does not feature in my lifetime cricketing statistics.

For the same reason neither should Louise's thirty-six runs, four wickets and blinding catch feature in hers.

14

THE NELSON TOUCH

There was a time when London pubs each had their own very distinct character. There were also thousands of them.

Their hours were almost universally 11a.m. to 3p.m. and then 5.30p.m. to 11p.m. (earlier closing on Sundays). These hours were sacrosanct unless there was some arcane byelaw as in places like Billingsgate or the old Covent Garden so that those working inhospitable hours could still get a drink. These places were useful to know if you were on a bender, and it was chucking out time where you were.

If you had a local pub and were considered affable enough by the host and others given this privilege, you would be allowed to stay on for 'afters'.

Often called a lock-in, this is the informal invitation, usually left unsaid, to stay behind after everyone else had been hustled out. The doors were then locked and the blinds drawn.

For some reason, 'afters' were always far more fun than the regular hours. It was not that the conversation was more stimulating, it certainly wasn't, or that great ideas were formed and problems solved, far from it. Indeed any sober stranger would have been pushed to make sense of most of what was uttered in that limbo time.

No, it was more the warmth of camaraderie, the ridiculous behaviour, absurd boasts and tales of humiliation that were shared between revellers while good and decent people went about their business or slept that made you feel you were somehow gaining time on the ordinary world. Nothing could have been further from the truth.

With experience came the knowledge that you were engaged in a complete waste of time and money while testing the patience of all those with whom you were in a relationship, your workmates and certainly your more responsible and long-suffering family and friends.

Inebriated, though, there was a shared sense that we were a brotherhood (and sisterhood, for the slurring female of the species was absolutely essential to these gatherings) of sozzled people. We loitered on the other side of the road most travelled by civilians, mocking in inebriated judgement what we took to be their dull existence.

It was a sort of drunks' snobbery, and it was very seductive until the ravages of ruined lives, bad temper and, of course, addiction, set in.

The character of these sessions was as individual as the pub they were held in and depended completely on the innkeeper and the regulars. In my 'afters' days, I enjoyed sporting drinking sessions, theatrical, artistic and literary ones, gay, straight and very peculiar ones and some 'afters' that were excessively violent and some that might have become amorous but for the condition of all those involved.

You could often feel the vibe of a pub the moment you walked in and, while some bore only the shortest scrutiny before you turned and fled, others felt like home almost immediately.

Very few of these pubs, as I would have recognised them, still exist in London and, some might argue sadly, even fewer have a set of regulars and their own unique character.

But, in the mid 1970s, you were spoilt for choice and the pub that I called my local for over three years in my early twenties, and which could not possibly exist now, was The Nelson.

It is hard now to believe that pubs in the more prosperous parts of the capital had a distinctly different clientele in their saloon bars to their public bars and that this lack of mingling was happily self-policed.

I discovered The Nellie, as we regulars called her, for she was a maternal and comforting place, quite by chance.

It was the height of summer and the Beauchamp Place street party was in full swing. These were events that smallish shopping lanes held during the season to promote sales and drive new punters into their shops.

It was not unlike a village fête, and you would end up having bought all sorts of useless and expensive things and eaten and drunk too much, all at an unsuitable time of day.

So it was, laden with impractical wares and not entirely sober, I set out to meet a new girlfriend at her parents' house nearby. I aimed to arrive there at six but, in my enthusiasm not to be late, I found myself only yards away with half an hour to kill.

It was then that I saw what, as first sight, looked like a smallish corner house in a short terrace, lost among the imposing houses of a great London square. These mansions all had mews houses and often staff quarters attached to them and stood in the isolated grandeur of their own existence with no shops or tradesmen to be seen.

I looked up at the ivy-covered, ancient building and nestling among the creepers was a sign bearing the unmistakable likeness of he of the immortal memory and, below this, his name; The Nelson.

The door was closed but I tried it, nonetheless.

It opened onto a tiny snug with, perhaps, five cushioned stools at the bar, a small table surrounded by a banquette and a couple of chairs. Another small table with a further couple of chairs stood by a fireplace. This was the Saloon Bar.

One wall of this nook was formed by a wood and glass screen with an arch let into it through which I could see much of what was obviously the Public Bar.

All the lights were off but sunlight streamed through the frosted windows and its beam fell on the figure of an oldish man laid out across two tables. His spectacles were askew, his trousers bunched around his ankles and a pair of very old-fashioned underpants were pulled high above his waist into which his shirt and the bottom of his tie were tucked. He had a neat moustache of the military kind, stained yellow on one side from years of nicotine. His cheeks were highly florid, his nose bulbous and his eyes were closed but, nonetheless flickered behind thickly lensed horn-rimmed glasses.

He looked very peaceful.

I was going to turn around and leave him to his evening sleep when a rather strangled voice said,

'Oi, you. Do you want a drink?'

'Who, me?' I asked.

'Yes, sir, you, Sir.'

He spoke in a way that, without knowing him, could either have been excessively polite or lightly ironic. When I got to know him better, I still had this same dichotomy as decades of hard boozing, a rich social life and, as he would often remind us, 'The Jungle' had left him prone to a febrile mix of moods, very often all displayed at the same time.

'I'd love one if it isn't a bore.' I answered.

'Not a bore, not a bore at all. What time is it?' He sat up and began to swivel around on one of the tables to put his feet on the ground which movement was complicated by the position of his trousers.

'Now what's going on here?' He said, looking down at his bare thighs. 'Where are my bloody trousers?' He patted his thighs.

'Around your ankles.' I said pointing at them.

140

'Well, that's no good.' He said, 'No good down there, they need to be up here.'

He muttered this as he pulled up his trousers and secured them around his waist with a thin piece of orange material, but they remained well below the top of his underpants whose label, sticking out of the back, bore the legend, Army & Navy Stores.

He turned unsteadily and, now that his eyes were open, I could see just how bloodshot and rheumy they were.

'Poison?' He asked, pulling up the flap in the bar to insinuate himself into the tiny area behind it.

So small was this space that he was almost under the optic as he pressed the glass that had appeared in his hand up and into the gin spigot. He pressed again and I was about to tell him that I didn't want gin when he pulled down the glass, put it to his lips and drained it all in one graceful movement.

He let out a long and loud sigh, weighted it seemed with a sense of inevitability as to how the next few hours would go.

'Poison?' He repeated.

'Could I have a glass of beer and a whisky, please? Bell's if you would' I asked. He raised an eyebrow.

'Large or small?' His eyebrow remained cocked.

'Large, please. I'll put in the water.' I added.

'Good man.' He uncocked his eyebrow, slid the glass over to me and said,

'I've given you the local beer...rest is filth.'

He passed across a straight-sided glass with an opaque mixture swirling around in it like the wake of a Thai market boat, spilling much of it as he did so.

'Oops, sorry about that. She normally pours the drinks.' He jerked his head vaguely upwards and towards some stairs that led up through a small, low door set into the corner of the tiny room.

He hitched his spectacles high on his forehead, leant his elbows on the bar and sighed mightily again.

'Local?' he asked, rolling his eyes up to me and, obviously seeing only a blur, pulled his glasses down again with a little moment of imbalance.

'Ah, there you are.' He said and shuffled his feet.

'Not really.' I said in answer to his question.

'Not really what?' he asked.

'Local.' I sensed that this disjointed conversation might easily last up to the time I had to leave and even far beyond.

'No, thought not. So, what brings you here?' He asked, rubbing one eye under his glasses.

'I am taking out a girl who lives round the corner and I'm a bit early.' I drank my whiskey at a gulp and took a small sip of the beer, which was my prevailing technique for the opening drink in those heady days.

Alan peered at me over the top of his glasses with some respect 'Good man.' He said. 'Another?'

I nodded my head and, as he squirted out my whisky, he helped himself to another large, neat gin.

'A girl, you say?' And he leant, confidentially towards me. 'Not Hairy Mary or one of those girls, is it?'

'I'm sorry?' I was confused.

'Over the road, the old brothel…not one of those girls.'

'No.' I replied.

He briefly tried to raise himself from his improbably relaxed leaning position but soon gave up.

'Good, you shouldn't really go in there unless you want something outlandish, thrashing, nanny stuff, buggery….that sort of thing. Terrible old tarts, though they're nice enough. Come in here sometimes, friendly girls.'

There was silence while he gazed at the bar and I took in this information.

'No.' I said, finally, 'She's not like that…well, I'm pretty sure, ha ha.'

But it was a hollow laugh and I felt I had not only insulted the prostitutes but somehow shown myself not to be a man of the world.

'Another?' He asked. I had drunk my whiskey without noticing. 'Why not?'

'Good man.' He said and performed the same double-handed trick as before.

No money had changed hands, nor been asked for, and I was beginning to worry that I would be landed with the tab for all our drinks thus far.

He slid my whiskey over to me, refilled the water jug from a tap under the counter, and said,

'Name?'

'Theo.' I replied.

'Aha, I knew a Theo in the Army.' and, after a momentary pause he asked, 'Any relation?'.

'Well probably not. Probably more likely if the surname was the same.' I tried not to sound patronising and so couched the reply as a question.

'Good point, good point.' He said, shaking his head. 'Can't remember his other name. Good man, though.'

Then I made a classic pub error. After all my pub hours I should have known so much better.

I was getting late, embroiled with a sot and beginning to get the flavour myself, but I still asked.

'So you were in the Army, then?'

He finally managed to raise himself from his slumped state, stubbed out his cigarette with ochre fingers into the overflowing ashtray, and looked into the middle distance.

'Chindits'. He said, getting as close to standing to attention as he could. 'Heard of them?'

'Certainly have.' I answered enthusiastically.

'Ghastly business.' He looked down at his empty glass. 'Simply ghastly.'

He suddenly took a huge breath in and seemed to snap himself out of his reverie and turned towards the optics again.

'Once more to the spigot?' He cried, and it was the very first time I heard him utter one of his singular expressions that was to become a familiar exhortation.

'Why not?' I answered.

'Why not, indeed?' He replied.

It was well past the time I had set for myself to leave in order to meet my date, my senses were beginning to hum and my mind was slipping into that gentle, softened state that the first drink after the last sensible one takes you.

All sense of responsibility and thoughts of the future, however immediate, were beginning to be swept away by Mr Bell's amber pacifier.

As he was preparing two more large ones, a few people started to make their desultory way into the tiny snug.

The public bar had been filling up nicely with what I took to be regulars, domestic staff from the big houses, drivers, shopworkers and such; an eclectic mix, who, as I was to learn, were terrific company.

The first few punters drifting into the saloon appeared to be somewhat raffish but well-to-do men from the City. Their well-cut suits, stiff collars and gleaming shoes, were part of the traditional uniform then of chaps who were 'something in the City'. But, in most of their cases, these clothes disguised a very different type altogether; the ne'er do well.

Despite the money, time, emotional fury and wasted effort consorting with members of this brotherhood of wasters has cost me, it still surprises me how much I enjoyed being with them.

From the moment I engaged these new acquaintances in conversation, I was entertained and, as other members of this motley crew arrived and the snug became full to bursting with smoke, laughter and bonhomie, I found each new addition as amusing as the last.

And motley they were.

I came to know them far too well over the next few years and not one of their voyages through life's ocean was anywhere near plain sailing. But, on that first night, I only had their immediate performances to judge by.

It was, by no means, a solely masculine or City group. A couple of middle-aged ladies who had arrived, raucous and sozzled from the street party, were given a small cheer as they walked in, followed by an old man who looked as if he had strayed from an Impressionist's garret with a small terrier that was immediately made much of by the whole room.

'If that fucking dog does that again, I'm shooting it.' Roared Alan.

'Boooo.' Roared the crowd followed by jeers and laughter.

The atmosphere was enchanted and each person who came in seemed friendlier than the last. The mix was heady but, in retrospect, alcohol and an addiction to it were our only real common denominators.

Looking back on my days of public house dissipation it is hard to recall what conversations could possibly have held my attention for up to, and sometimes beyond, six hours. I seemed to learn a lot from the most diverse of people but, on considered reflection, I can't remember a single useful thing.

They did, however, teach me how to converse with anyone about almost anything, even if I had no idea what I was talking about, and this has proved of untold value in my life, even in sobriety.

I came to know all these people's histories, or at least the ones they put forward, and one or two wonderful friendships were formed in The Nelson.

One of the future friends I met that night was Andrew who, a couple of years later, made the great mistake of asking me to be his best man. I arrived for this celebration, coincidentally after a night at The Nelson, a good hour and a half after I was meant to have made my speech.

My arrival was greeted with ribald laughter by most and terrific *laissez-faire* by Andrew. His mother and father, however, were not amused at all and I was admonished by the Brigadier with the words,

'If you're the best man my son could find then there is no hope for him.'

His father's lack of confidence was borne out as Andrew shot himself some years later, the victim of a truly promising life ruined by drink. He was extremely intelligent and kind; his senseless death gave many of us pause but not, alas, pause enough to give up drinking.

A couple more of the regulars will feature elsewhere in these ramblings but take my word for it, the crowd in there was a heady brew.

My first night there I had been refusing as many drinks as I accepted but, even so, by the time I had pulled myself together, I was a good hour and a half late for my date and not in a condition to show myself in my best light.

My new comrades were imploring me to stay, habitual behaviour for inebriates as I had long since discovered, as they rarely have anywhere to go and little chance of getting there as all their bridges have been burned.

I explained about my new girlfriend, that I was enamoured of her and already very late, which merely increased their efforts to make me stay. I turned finally to leave the warm bosom of their friendship.

I sought out Alan, and said,

'Alan, I must be off.' I noticed my speech had become noticeably slurred.

'Good man, splendid.' He answered, 'we'll see you soon, I hope.'
'I owe you for my drinks.' I said, dreading the bill.

'Not a bit, not to worry, we'll sort something out when you're next in.'

He put his arm around my shoulders. 'But that may be ages.' I said.

'Oh, I think not.' He said and slapped my back. 'Good man.'

This sent me lurching into the somewhat unexpected daylight and it felt a little unhealthy, not to say wasteful, to be in that a state on such a glorious summer evening.

I walked the short distance to my date's house and rang the bell.

I was swaying from foot to foot in a nervous little dance and practising my first, apologetic sentence out loud to myself when the door opened and a tall, distinguished-looking and very neat gentleman with carefully brushed silver hair opened it.

'Yeeees?' He drawled, 'And you are?'

'Theo, Sir, m'here to….' was as far as I got before he asked.

'Are you drunk, young man?'

'No, Sir, certainly not, Sir.' I protested but even to my own ears I could understand his suspicion. Then a disembodied girl's voice called loudly from the bowels of the house.

'Is that him?' It asked.

'Yes, indeed it is, and he's drunk.' The man shouted back.

I put my hand up and tried to look both sober and hurt. Judging by his expression as he looked me up and down, I wasn't succeeding.

'Tell him to go away.' The voice said.

'Right ho. You heard her, she wants you to go away.'

I started to say something but realised that my cause was lost when he put up his hand and said,

'Hup, 'up, 'up...that's enough, off you go and, if you ever want to come back again, I suggest you arrive on time, sober and not dressed like a tramp.'

'Fair enough.' I said and turned tail.

Even in that sodden state I was still very disappointed in myself, in my condition and, of course, losing out on an evening that I had been looking forward to.

I had let myself down.

Still, I thought, the night was young.

Retracing my tracks took me back to the Nelson.

Why not, I thought.

I opened the door and the raucous noise stopped immediately. Alan held up a hand for complete silence, looked over to me and said,

'That was quick, what happened?'

'She told me to fuck off.' I said.

The bar erupted; it was as if I had brought unexpected news of a great victory back to the Motherland.

Alan rang the bell,

'Drinks!' he shouted, squirting out a large Bell's, and my back was slapped as I pushed through to the bar.

'I said you'd be back.' He gurned.

I had found my local.

15

Bodily Malfunctions

I had a debate with myself – not something I always win – as to whether the acute embarrassments caused by our traitorous bodies should be included in this collection of calamities.

The civilised world is fairly divided into those who find anything to do with the body or its functions both abhorrent and vulgar and then others, perhaps of a more childish disposition, who enjoy nothing more than lurid stories of their own or other people's corporal malfunctions.

I fall very much into the latter category.

So, for all those of you in the former, please turn to the next chapter.

Of all the humiliations to which my body has subjected me, and my flesh has been heir to many, the most comprehensively mortifying was having a Barium enema.

The procedure itself is obviously of huge importance and must be had by those who need it, so I do not want my experience to act as a deterrent but merely a cautionary tale. It is not painful and leads to proper diagnostics which, in turn, often lead to great relief, cures and, perhaps, even the saving of life.

I first had this process when I was in my twenties and it only led to a very banal diagnosis requiring a change of diet, after which much discomfort and embarrassment was exorcised.

I hadn't really listened to my doctor or read the instructions that accompanied the kit I was given. I just mixed and drank some filthy liquid at home which caused a sudden and comprehensive vacating of my bowels so I spent the day and night before the enema in a watery-eyed and ever more weakened state at home, easily within lurching distance of a loo.

Despite my youth, I arrived at the hospital in a diminished and pathetic state but determined to be of good cheer and take it all as manfully as possible.

I was asked to don one of those absurd surgical gowns, always too short and never meeting at the back, which further tested my resilience, and then to walk down to a room which appeared to be the command deck of a lunar rocket launch.

There were two young nurses chatting together, discussing their coming weekend, and they barely registered my entrance. After a few minutes of waiting, one of them turned around and smiled professionally at me. I smiled back and, as the other turned, I tried to engage them in conversation.

It is difficult to feel in any way confident when your body has been drained of almost everything and you are standing in cellophane slippers and a thin cotton slip with your bottom hanging out for the world to see, trying to pull the front down to cover the end of your frightened willy.

Nonetheless I turned to one of them with a dry-mouthed grin. 'Hello,' I said, 'and what do you do?'

'I'm a nurse.' She answered simply.

There was a hiatus while they looked at each other and I felt it fruitless to ask the other nurse what she did.

'Oh, ah.' I blurted, 'What sort?'

It seemed the only *sequitur* available.

'The sort that sticks a tube up your bottom.' She said, smiling.

Nothing in my past had really equipped me for how to continue this niche banter so I adopted what I felt to be a manly and insouciant pose and said to the other.

'What a lovely day.'

'Except for the rain.' She answered.

'Yes, apart from that....' I paused.

'Doing anything special this weekend?' I asked, but I immediately realised that it sounded like a chat-up line, so I added,

'I am.' I realised that I was neither looking my best nor being amusing and I was losing ground fast. As often happened, I had no idea why I wanted to ingratiate myself with people who I would never see again and with whom no conversation was expected or required. I was certainly not hoping for special treatment as I had no idea what was in store apart from the aforementioned tube.

They looked at each other and then one said, 'Oh, so what's that?'

'What's what?' I asked.

'What you're doing this weekend.'

I had forgotten I'd mentioned that I was 'doing something' at the weekend merely to cover my earlier embarrassment and so I floundered a bit.

'Just stuff, really.' I answered and couldn't even imagine what a tit they must have thought me.

I tried to smile winningly.

'Sorry, I'm babbling.' I said and sat on the edge of a machine.

The very cold corner of it seemed to be trying to force its way between my buttocks and I realised I might slip onto it, when one of the nurses cried out.

'Not there.' I leapt up, 'That's sterile.'

This caused me some confusion.

'Oh, sorry,' I said.

'Don't worry.' The other nurse said soothingly, 'It's nerves. Everyone gets a bit fluttery before this process.'

'Oh, I'm not nervous at all,' I said, trying to look strong and cool, 'Just want to get it over with.'

They squinted suspiciously at me.

I was, in fact, beginning to get more than a bit twitchy and realised they must have seen this sort of skittish behaviour a thousand times before and I really wasn't impressing them at all when, thankfully, the doctor walked in.

'Morning.' He boomed. 'All ready to go?'

'Yes, he won't need a sedative, he's fine.' One of the nurses said.

'That's the spirit.' The doctor said with a grin.

No-one had actually offered me a sedative.

I knew this as I love sedatives and strongly believe that things go much better with them, but the nurses had obviously decided to play me at my own game.

I realised that I now needed to appear brave throughout.

I was strapped onto a sort of rocking gurney and asked to pull one leg up. Adopting this position meant that any remaining vestige of hope I still nurtured of impressing the nurses disappeared. One of them prepared me with Vaseline and then inserted a tube while I lay like an immobile beetle flinching and gasping at every movement of her hand. The other toyed with some machine and I began to fill with what appeared to be air.

My stomach extended like a pale, pink lilo and I feared that, if the nozzle came loose, I might fly around the surgery like a balloon, emitting some hideous and shameful noise, only to wrap myself, deflated, around a chair.

Then I felt the strange sensation of something being poured into me. I was trying not to look at the nurses as they were working with their faces very close to my privates. The gown was now above my stomach so I was visually unprotected, and I feared that, at any moment, such were the strange sensations, that a loss of control might cause some terrible accident and ruin the nurses' weekend and even persuade them to question their calling.

Lodged into this position, feeling as you might if you were dying to pee while sitting in the middle of the front row at a very quiet and serious play, they began to rotate me.

The doctor pointed out on a screen the Barium going into my colon and stomach and other places, but I was too intent on not letting myself down or exploding in front of the nurses. Indeed, I was still trying to rustle up a nonchalant grin each time our faces met during my rotations.

This seemed to go on for a very long time, new pressures and positions were explored as my distended stomach appeared to be getting ever nearer to bursting, while the doctor pointed out things of interest in my insides muttering the occasional 'That's good' or 'Hmm'.

I had lost all interest in what the diagnosis might be while my miserable lower half lay revealed for the nurses to be repelled by.

In this enfeebled position, a deep thought penetrated my consciousness. I was actually more interested in not looking foolish in the eyes of the nurses than I was about the seriousness of what ailment this examination might reveal.

I tried to think myself into a more sensible state of mind when the rocking stopped.

'There we are.' Said the surgeon as the machinery ran itself to a stop and a humming silence reigned.

I waited for instructions.

''All done.' Said one of the nurses. 'I'll just get this off.' And she removed the tube. I braced myself for the imagined wind-powered spin around the surgery, but nothing happened. There was still something there and it was uncomfortable to move.

I tried to stand normally.

'Sorry, what now?' I said, rearranging my gown.

'You'll want to go and vacate your bowels now.' Said the doctor and one of the nurses handed me a very small towel.

'Follow me.' She said, leading me to a door in the corner of the room.

This opened to a cubicle that had another door at right angles in it opposite a loo. Behind this I could quite clearly hear people talking. I threw the nurse a quizzical look.

'The waiting room.' She said, adding

'When you're finished just go out of that door and collect your clothes where you left them. OK?'

'Oh,' I said, 'Can I just go then?'

'Unless you feel a bit groggy…some people feel a bit giddy after having all that stuff pushed into them.'

'Do they?' I asked.

'Yes, but I don't suppose you'll be one of those.' She said but I detected no irony.

What could she mean? Was it because I was such a fine physical specimen that she assumed I could take this sort of bodily invasion or, what seemed more likely, that my stomach looked well able to take on board the extra gallons of liquid?

With this conundrum dangling and aware that I still had something inserted, I asked her, pointing behind me,

'What about this?'

'Oh, heavens.' She said looking around to see if the doctor had noticed, 'Quite right, I'll just get that out. When I do, hold it all in as much as you can till you get above the toilet, won't you?' She said, biting her bottom lip.

'I hate this bit.' She added, somewhat unnecessarily.

She took me to the gurney, bent me over with a sort of large kidney bowl under me and gently pulled the plug out.

I waited again for the flatulent trip around the surgery but still nothing happened.

'There you go, quickly now.' She said, and I waved over my shoulder hoping to catch both of their eyes, but they were turned away waiting for the next patient.

I waddled to the door in the corner and locked it behind me. It was a very sterile loo and full of those mysterious contraptions that you only see in hospital lavatories covered in frightening pictures of razor blades and syringes with vivid red crosses over them.

As I lowered myself nervously onto the cold plastic seat, I could clearly hear a couple talking over the general hubbub and conversation of a full waiting-room, they were only two feet in front of me. The door afforded absolutely no soundproofing or privacy at all, it was as if I were in the room next to them.

Then, from nowhere, whatever ghastly potion they had filled me with and a Zeppelin's worth of air, both having been kept under appalling pressure for nearly an hour, exploded like a Texas oil strike from my bottom.

The noise was both ear-splitting and inhuman, the first salvo silenced the entire waiting room immediately. A short, ringing silence ensued and then people suddenly began to talk in shocked voices all at once.

'Fucking hell, what was that?' was the first recognisable remark, but then other shocked voices started to join in and ask each other just what in the name of God the noise might have been.

'Accident?' Suggested one, 'Electrical?'

'Nah, sounded more like ...' and, at that moment I started again and this unstoppable wind, with the occasional remnant of the Barium concoction, continued to expel itself like a savage tropical storm for what seemed the lifetime of a small mammal.

A few shouts of dismay and disbelief – tinged with a little terror – began to make themselves heard during this second movement but most of the waiting room had been stunned into silence.

It was as if they had been struck down, in awe at being present during a rare, pagan, but natural phenomenon – something like a tornado twinned with a witches' Sabbath.

It seemed to me that it would never stop and, each time I thought the end was nigh, it started again. Finally, weeping tears of defeat, I began to run out of puff, as it were.

I was now hollow and utterly enfeebled, my eyes stinging, and my body shaking and spent. I tried to clean myself up as best as I could with the unabsorbant materials to hand and pulled the lever on the cistern which bore the command 'flush' which my face obeyed.

The murmur of chat the other side of the door fell to silence as worry replaced wonder. As there was no sound from beyond the surgery door and no-one asking if I needed help, I took it that my experience was normal, however unlikely that seemed.

I pressed the lever again as it had malfunctioned but, before anything could happen, I realised that the earlier sound and fury had signified almost nothing, so I immediately had to sit down again.

When I was sure, and this was after some considerable time, that I was safe to leave the cubicle, I had to steel myself to walk into the waiting room, still in the short gown with my beleaguered arse hanging out, through the very audience that had just witnessed, aurally if not visually, my shameful storm.

I unlocked the door and turned the knob; complete silence fell.

I tried to look casual, but I was quite unsteady on my legs and my smile might have appeared somewhat wan.

I noticed a few people muttering to each other and one or two nodding towards me, as they might have towards a witch, recognising the contriver of the previous ten minutes' inhuman cacophony. Some actually flinched as I passed.

I stumbled to the locker where I found my clothes and put them on as quickly as I could.

Too quickly, it transpired, as there was still a little vacating to do. Then, when I was finally dressed, I realised I had to walk back through the waiting room.

I wanted to do so with my head held high, despite the humiliation of the last minutes, and in a debonair and jaunty manner.

In the corridor, before I reached the waiting room, I heard one of my nurses engaged in conversation with some of the sitting patients.

'But that can't be normal, surely nurse?' One was saying, 'I mean that was frightening!''I thought he was going to explode.' Another said and then an old lady piped up,

'I'm surprised his bum didn't fall off.' Everyone laughed.

'Well, that was a really good one, I'll give you that.' Said the nurse. 'We don't get many like that maybe one a month, but the funny thing is that, normally the really noisy ones are absolute sweethearts.'

'What about this one?' Asked the old lady.

'No, a bit of a tit, actually.' She said as I strode into the room trying my best to look like a sweetheart.

16

ON THE SLIPPERY SLOPE

I am not a huge fan of organised winter sports, the kind you travel abroad to indulge in, and I haven't been since first I tried it in the faraway fifties.

Skiing and its winter cousins then were unrecognisable from today's brash and crowded versions. There were very few places to ski, very few people did it and the clothes were dark, elegant and understated. Much tweed and flannel was in evidence.

The kit was rudimentary. Skis were ultra-long and hand-made from wood, boots were laced up and made of leather, as were the gloves, and the bindings were unreliable and had no safety fastenings.

Lifts were few and far between and the original pick-axe versions were almost impossible to stay on especially if a much taller adult had a child on the other side.

This meant that, more often than not, we had to climb up a hill, either carrying our long and heavy skis in unwaterproofed boots or struggle up the slope, parallel ski to parallel ski, both of which methods were slow, incredibly tiring and deeply dull.

You were always either very hot or very, very cold and I cannot remember ever being able to get the laces on my ski boots undone at the end of a day's skiing.

I snapped a ligament in my knee on one of these trips when I was about nine and returned to school with the whole leg, from ankle to thigh, in plaster. After the initial novelty of my co-students seeing it and having related the tale of derring-do that caused it endlessly, I was left with a few autographs on it and a hole I had drilled through it to scratch the almost permanent itch above my knee.

I had to lie with it horizontal while listening to the pock of ball on bat from outside waiting for the great day it was to be cut off. When this happened, my leg floated upwards, as I had been warned it would, unused to the lack of weight as I vowed I would never ski again.

It didn't put me off other snow and ice-related sports and in the unbelievably hard winter of 1963 as all games were cancelled, we had to make do with tobogganing on tin trays and running at an ice-packed downhill path and sliding down it on leather-soled shoes.

There were many crashes and much blood spilt but I these sports were never overseen by teachers or stopped.

My avoidance of skiing lasted until my early twenties, when I began to go out with a girl who was a fabulous, highly-skilled and very brave skier.

I had told her I'd sworn off skiing but, as the choice was staying at home and letting her ski amongst infamously randy ski instructors and slope-bashers or to accompany her and her family, I decided to go.

It was a bad choice.

For reasons I cannot now comprehend, I assumed I would be, at the very least, a proficient skier and maybe a natural.

For all sorts of reasons, I discovered I was not.

I liked to think that my long legs didn't suit a sport where a low centre of gravity was an advantage, and, that I wasn't used to the new equipment.

I also soon realised that tweed was no longer cool on the slopes.

Skiing with her was as impossible as it would have been playing tennis with Federer so we would meet for lunch. This would come after I had fallen off a few lifts, been humiliated by children and tried to master the Jet turn – quite a change from the Stem Christiana and the Snow Plough of my youth.

I skied a few more times with her and then we went our separate ways. I hung up my skis while she stayed on the slopes where she lives to this day.

But winter sports had a few surprises left for me. For reasons I still cannot credit, I went on a holiday to Zermatt with my friend Johnnie, who appears elsewhere in these pages, and an older and eccentric couple, who were magnificent skiers, a girlfriend and a couple of others.

It became obvious that Johnnie and I were the rabbits of the party so we would get up late, ski gently until we met the others for a long lunch, and then ski home while they conquered new mountains.

The ski down was always a difficult one as we would both have had too much lunch and one day I was flattened by a Japanese gentleman on a snowboard, both then rarities and unusual sights on the pistes.

I was knocked senseless and a doctor was called who diagnosed concussion and charged Johnnie with taking me back to the chalet and keeping me awake at all costs. I was to eat and drink nothing and, if I was still dizzy or nauseous two hours later, to call him.

My old friend had obviously misunderstood the instructions and got me home and filled me with whiskey while we played a game which involved trying to stack all the furniture onto one sofa.

I then passed out and awoke when everyone returned to find Johnnie asleep.

I didn't feel dizzy or nauseous, so my minder had flown in the face of medical theory and shown there was another way.

Our behaviour through this short trip had been childish, I fear, some of it involving the local constabulary, and ended with an unfortunate incident with a sort of snow-trailer thing.

Zermatt had no cars in those days, perhaps still hasn't, so people and things were moved around on electric trollies with a little cab at the front to drive in and a flat back that you could sit on with your feet dangling down and put your skis, equipment or shopping on.

Johnnie and I had been ticked off both inside and outside the chalet by the local authorities for poor behaviour and we were on a warning; of what we weren't quite sure, but we were trying to behave ourselves.

Sadly, leaving a nightclub the evening of my concussion, we spotted one of these vehicles parked and open by the side of the road. It was too much to resist, so we boarded the beast and looked around for some sort of key or button but only succeeded in taking off the brake. It started to slide across the road and gather pace. Trying to put the brake back on did little to slow our progress on the icy road as we began to pick up pace over to the other side, where it bumped up onto the shallow pavement and towards the huge plate glass window of a ski-hire shop.

We abandoned the brute before the collision but slipped on landing and were both prone when it happened.

The noise was titanic in that crisp mountain air and brought a sudden crowd onto the previously deserted streets. I would say, in our defence that, in the darkness the damage looked worse than it turned out to be in the very cold light of day.

We were in no position to run for it on what was a skating rink under our feet and a very surly and official man arrived by our sides as we stood up.

'Zo!' He said, 'Zo, it is you two, zee Englishmen.......again.' It was our friend the local policeman with his sidekick, dressed in stone grey outfits and furry hats which bore their official badges on them. It was a faintly ludicrous look and, along with our refreshed state, took away a lot of the threat they were trying to impart with their stance, feet wide apart and their hands gripping their belts.

We were let off with another yellow card but warned that the slightest further infringement would have dire consequences. We had no idea what these might be either but we calmed down for a day or two and then something, and I forget what, as does Johnnie, led to us being asked, very politely, to leave Zermatt.

On the morning of our departure, we were shadowed by the two policemen who approached us on the railway platform for a chat as we waited for our train. They were obviously relieved to see us go but seemed to want to clear the air.

'I am zorry eet has come to zees.' He said ruefully, 'Zermatt vas put on zer map by zer Eenglish.' He shuffled his feet, looking down, and then raised his head to look us both in the eye.

'Vimper unt zer mountaineers, der skiiers unt zer uzzer vinter sports, vould not hef heppened but for zer Eenglish.' He sighed. 'In my time here, I hef only hed, vat you call ze bad run in viz one ozzer Eenglishman. Now you make zree.'

In the silence that followed we all looked at each other, he with disappointment and us with a slight sense of having let Blighty down a bit.

To break this hiatus I asked,

'And who was that?'

Unexpectedly, he gave us the name and, when I heard it, I was astounded. As was he when I blurted out,

'Good Lord, he's my cousin!' The train arrived before we could discuss this further.

After that, Louise and I went winter sporting only a couple of times, both unintended and both unfortunate.

One of these trips was to a friend's birthday weekend on which the behaviour became extremely messy.

It may hold unfortunate memories for some so I will not expand too much on it other than to mention this episode.

We had a handful of members of the various British bob teams in our party, and a few Cresta riders besides. Both of these activities are senseless and dangerous and to be avoided by sensible people. Mercifully the Cresta was deemed too risky for those of our number that hadn't done it, especially as a few of our team were exceptionally overweight, and we also had a man who was paralysed from the waist down.

For strange reasons it was not considered risky for us debutants to try the two-man bob, acting as brake-men behind the international drivers.

This is a strange sport and doesn't appear to have much science to it, other than the design of the bob itself which is built to go as fast as possible down a sheer, ice-track.

The brake-man's job is to run and push the bob, as I am sure you will all have seen, and then jump in once the vehicle is under way. The man who does this is normally a very hefty ex-sprinter or the like. Once on board, he adopts the foetal position, making himself as aerodynamic as he can and pulls two levers, one at either side of him, when the driver screams 'brake'.

This role may well require huge strength and agility in the real thing, but we were all mercifully put into the still bob and, when sitting, pushed gently off until gravity did the rest. This obviously made the ride slower.

We arrived at the hut at the top of the bob run having had a quite a few nerve-strengthening drinks and continued with these in the hut. A very officious man then wanted confirmation that we had all done the bob before and that none of us had had a drink. We all affirmed this to be the case and then we signed a piece of paper acknowledging that those in charge of the run had no responsibility for us.

I felt rather like the Kamikaze lads getting their last drop of sake and being told they were off in a minute.

I certainly had the divine wind up.

My driver was a very experienced cresta and bob rider having represented GB many times. He was also a bit mad, as you have to be, and not the best explainer of what we were about to do, relying mainly on arm gestures and schoolboy noises, rather like a teenage fighter pilot might have explained his first dog-fight.

I vaguely understood about the brakes and not to be too severe on them and to lean the way I was forced by centrifugal force, or was it the other way?

Otherwise I was in the dark.

I remained that way because, when I put on my crash-helmet, I discovered that it had clearly been made for the man who had won the world's biggest head competition and not only fell down over my eyes, but was extraordinarily heavy and wobbled from side to side like bucket on a stick.

I tried to tilt it towards the back of my head but this just pulled it back to face the sky.

I didn't want to whinge amongst these Übermenschen about an ill-fitting helmet and so I found I'd missed the start of the pair who went before us, both of whom were experts.

We had all been told to listen to what they said and then watch them carefully, as they knew what they were doing, and then do as exactly what they did.

Sadly, I had missed this demonstration as I had been consigned to the dark and silent world that was the inside of my elephantine helmet.

They were thundering down the run and out of sight.

My pilot walked over to our bob and squeezed himself into its nose and hunched himself over as if he meant business. I was helped into the back and a bar of some sort was pulled up against the side. The person who had helped me in gave me the thumbs up and began gently to push the sledge.

My driver turned around, apparently to give me some last-minute unintelligible instructions, but that was the last I saw or heard of him as my wretched helmet fell back down over my face as we picked up speed.

I fumbled for the brake handles and found something but didn't know if what I was clutching were they.

Anyone who has been on a particularly alarming ride at a funfair or amusement park will know that sensation of roaring and screeching noise, accompanied by the grotesque torque of being hurled around against the way your body wants to go by a force far greater than life has prepared for you, which raises fear, excitement and nausea in equal measure.

This was similar except your belief is that the fairground ride has been carefully checked by Health and Safety people and has not had even the slightest accident for decades whereas the toboggan you are in is being driven down a track, on which people actually have died, by a nutter trying to get down the fastest and riskiest way.

I can't tell you much more about the descent than the noise and the sensation because of my helmet but, when I lifted it we were in the blinding white of snow all around us, and had come to a more sudden halt than I had expected.

It was dazzling to a man who had spent the previous minutes in his own, dark world and we were tangled up in some sort of orange netting.

I leant back and my driver started to berate me in a fairly jovial way.

'What the fuck?' He gasped, 'Why didn't you brake when I said brake?'

'I didn't hear anything.' I said, trying to get myself out of the sledge which he had done with elegant ease from a more difficult position.

'I couldn't see anything either, my bloody helmet was over my eyes and ears.' I explained.

'Oh no!' He slapped his forehead with the palm of his hand like a cartoon character. 'So you missed everything…well, we'll do it again, I'm sure there's time.' My heart sank. I had made it down in one piece and had gained some bragging rights over those ingénues who hadn't accepted the offer of a ride, but the idea of doing it again, even in a well-fitting helmet, was not welcome.

I struggled out of the bob like a very old man extracting himself from a bean bag.

Our bob was dragged away as we walked up and over to the finish line, which I now noticed was some distance from the end of the run-out area and this was quite a long way from where we had finished up.

My lack of braking had obviously extended our journey and I was glad my helmet-blindness had shielded me from this episode.

'Let's watch the others come in.' He said.

Moments later there was an ominous rumble and an empty bob, on its side and at a novel angle, came rumbling down the track towards us.

It was a sombre sight and it made an eerie noise as it slowed past us and came to a halt like a spectre.

A moment later, one of the amateurs came slowly around the corner, half sliding, half kneeling and arrived at the bottom in some distress. They had flipped their bob over and his driver had lifted himself out of the track leaving his virginal brake-man to slide down on his back, bottom and, on occasion, knees to the finish where he made a wretched sight.

His jersey and shirt had all but disintegrated and his flesh was flayed, as were the better part of his buttocks. His knees and thighs were weeping with blood and whatever that stuff is that comes out apart from blood when you graze yourself.

He was not a pretty sight, but he was now very sober.

He was taken somewhere to be looked after but I don't think he missed much more of the weekend. I do know there was much healing of his body to get through when he got back to England.

Two more bobs came down without incident and my driver and I were about to go back to the top to do our second run when a bob came hurtling around the last bend at high speed and no obvious signs of slowing down but with a noise, even louder than the sledge itself, of human wailing.

It shot past us and buried itself in a tangle of orange netting in a snowdrift.

It was impossible to tell who this might have been, clothed as they both were in their kit, and when we got to the pile of clothing and metal in the snowdrift the first face we saw, as he removed his helmet, was one paralysed friend. He was beaming behind his raised visor and trying to raise himself on his elbows.

His driver pulled himself from the drift and bent down to help him, roaring with laughter.

He had started to drag the immobile man away from the bob when an official came strutting up towards him. He had obviously been made aware that the last half a dozen runs, our slots, had ended in various farcical and dangerous ways and had been sent down to find out why.

He walked over to the prostrate man and his driver, who he obviously knew well but didn't think much of.

'What is going on, who are these people?' He swung his arm around taking us all in.

'These are my friends.' He said, smiling. 'We're just celebrating a birthday.'

'Well, you need to all get out of the way and clear this area. We have more riders to come so please move.' He said emphatically and looked down at the prone man.

'You.' He said. 'Get up and move, quickly, please, quickly.'

'I can't.' He said, trying to roll onto his side.

'Why not, why not, what is wrong, are you drunk?'

By this time the Swiss gentleman was getting very cross and the fact that we were all so obviously bubbling with mirth angered him even more.

'Why not!' He stamped his foot.

'Because I'm fucking paralysed.' He shouted and we all burst into uncontrollable laughter.

I felt sorry for the official, but he was in no way placated when things were explained to him. Our friend had fulfilled his ambition, but we were forbidden any more runs.

I almost cried with relief.

17

GOING DOWNHILL

My very last ski trip with Louise was both unplanned and unwanted.

At a time when we were completely broke, some years into our marriage but before our children were born, we were asked to a charity event. Some very well-off friends had taken a table and asked us to join them.

This sort of invitation provided one of our best sources of the good nourishment so important to a young body and we were inclined to say yes to these events unless the cause was so much against our principles – and I cannot remember that happening – or the hosts were so boring or awful that we preferred to eat pot noodles at home, and this did happen quite a bit.

Our threshold was pretty low, however, so we did go to quite a a lot of these things.

Our hosts at this particular event were a very charming and roguish couple that we saw a lot of at the time and who were mad keen skiers.

The party followed the usual course and, after some speeches, an auctioneer took to the podium and began to sell the strange things that you would almost never consider buying, doing or owning, were it not for charity.

Having absolutely no money at the time any fun, as it is for us and for most people, was in watching the vanity of the rich people in the room as they competed to drive up the prices.

One of the lots was the use of a ski chalet in *Val d'Isère* for a week for two people and, as our hosts nudged each other, I could see they were keen. I rolled my eyes at Louise as the bidding started.

It rose very slowly as it was one of those difficult lots that demand you choose a date from a tight window in the calendar and share the chalet with others, so it was really only for the ski nut.

As the bidding stopped, I suddenly felt my arm being raised. The auctioneer saw this and took my bid and, as I looked around to see who had done this, the hammer came down and I was the owner of a week in the Alps.

Malcolm laughed.

'Oh, no?' Louise groaned. 'What are you doing? We can't even pay the fucking electricity bill?' Then she burst into tears.

Other than sentimental tears at films and very occasionally of anger, I had never seen her cry. Tears of disappointment are hard to cope with, especially when aimed at you. She had stood firm like a trooper, in the face of our unbelievably rackety finances for years but this was the obvious limit.

I had rarely seen her so upset.

I looked at Malcolm and said.

'It's really not funny. We're absolutely brassic and we're up to our neck in bills.' He regarded me, a nervous smile on his face, to see if I was joking. His face straightened as he began to realise I wasn't. 'Have you ever seen Louise like this?' I asked him.

'Really? Really, Christ, I had no idea.' He said. 'I'll sort something out, don't worry. I'll sort it out, but you two have to come skiing with us.'

What he sorted out, though generous, was far from ideal.

He paid off my bid, only fair as he had instigated it, and then, later in the week, booked an all-in holiday at an hotel in *Val d'Isère* for the four of us.

It was not as well-meant as it seemed as he really just wanted some company on yet another of his skiing holidays and neither Louise nor I wanted to go anywhere near the place; the idea of a forced skiing holiday with two mad-keen skiers filled us both with horror.

We also knew, experienced liggers that we were, that the incidentals, *abonnements*, ski-hire, drinks and food would be punishing and we had no way of paying as we were hugely overdrawn at the time, a fairly constant state of affairs for the first decade and more of our marriage.

Credit cards didn't exist, nor did cashpoints, so withdrawing cash from the bank or traveller's cheques were the only tender available, unless the person you were paying was trusting enough to accept your cheque. Flying a kite, as it was known, was always tempting and offered a short-term solution to lack of liquidity, but it was dangerous and deeply stressful as you had to get the money to the bank before your cheque (kite) was presented.

Being abroad gave you a bit more leeway but you could still only pay for stuff rather than get out cash and, in a cash-dominated world as it then was, it left you unable to pay for all sorts of vital things...like drink, ciggies and, well almost anything.

We saw an awkward time ahead and Louise remained deeply dubious about the whole piece of chicanery right up to the moment we left.

We were not a happy four as we arrived in the Alps. The old girlfriend I mentioned earlier in the chapter lived in the town and she suddenly appeared in the place we had chosen for dinner, which was not ideal, and she led my host and me around the drinking spots of the town long after our wives had decided to go back to the hotel.

Malcolm and I got back very late and very drunk indeed. I decided just to take my shoes off and sleep on top of the bed so as not to wake Louise.

This was handy because what turned out to be two hours later I was woken by Malcolm's angry wife, Jo, informing me that she had met a ski guide the night before and had booked him to take her husband and me up onto the fresh snow over the other side of the mountains and we needed to get going right now.

'Wha, wd, hmm?' I remember saying.

Louise had woken up and had a beatific smile on her face.

I smiled back at her, but I began to realise that her smile was not aimed at a wretchedly hung-over and smelly man that had come home very late, probably woken her up but definitely left the tap running in the bathroom and knocked over her sponge bag, spreading its contents across the bathroom floor and then trampled them into the tiles.

No, it was because she had been there when Jo booked this man to take us skiing somewhere high and cold and way beyond her husband's capabilities. She knew that I was going to be dragged up a mountain in the dark and freezing early morning to the top of a hill on which I might well lose my life.

That's why she was smiling.

I dressed as best I could and, not having much in the way of ski clothes, made do with some long johns, two pairs of socks, old tweed breeches, many jerseys and an anorak which was my only real skiing article apart from gloves. I was missing appropriate underwear and a hat, but I did have some goggles with yellow lenses that I remembered made the world look a happy place when I had last worn them.

I wandered down with Malcolm, who was dressed for the Olympics, to a sort of changing room in the basement which was packed with ski-kit. I had no idea what my hired kit looked like or which my locker was but he told me it would all be in a sort of frame under my room number.

This didn't help as I had no idea what my room number was, so I assumed it would be close to his and tried on various boots until

I found some that fitted and took those with the accompanying skis and sticks.

The skis were so short compared to what I had been used to that I thought I had taken some poor child's but then noticed that Malcolm's were the same length.

'I haven't got a hat.' I said to him in an unrecognisable voice.

'No need.' He croaked back, 'No need hat, hot, sunny.' He pointed at the ceiling. 'Sunny.' He repeated.

We hobbled towards the exit with that ridiculous walk that ski boots inflict on you and peered out into the freezing, indigo morning.

At the bottom of the black-iced stairs outside the hotel, languishing against the wall, was a shambles of a man dressed as something between a bomber pilot and an unsuccessful folk singer.

He was smoking a joint.

He picked a bit of tobacco off the front of his tongue and rolled his eyes up towards us and, with a slow, spreading grin said.

'You Malcolm and someone?' We nodded and he slung his skis over his shoulder and set off up the dark road.

'I'm your guide.' He tossed the words back at us. 'Bill. He added, and called out,

'This way.'

He walked up the short hill towards the lifts with an easy and athletic step in his ski-boots that left us clumping in his wake, struggling doubly with our savage hangovers.

Almost at once my ears started to burn with cold and I regretted listening to Malcolm about not needing a hat and whined to Joe.

'My ears are freezing. I need to go back and get a hat.'

Bill stopped with a sigh and a shrug.

'Ain't got time.' He said and pulled a large piece of cloth out of his jacket pocket.

As he flicked this around to form a strip, I noticed it was the Stars and Stripes which seemed to clear up the matter of his nationality as he had sounded both American and Australian.

He bound this around my ears like a hippie bandana which somewhat clashed, culturally, with my tweed trousers.

We got onto a chair lift, Malcolm on his own, leaving me to share a seat with Bill.

After an embarrassing mix-up while mounting the chair, during which I both poked myself in the eye with one of my ski-sticks and let my skis slide out of my hands and fall onto Bill's shoulders quite hard, we settled down for the long ride to the top.

Bill fired up another joint and offered me a puff.

I declined as I already felt appalling and feared it might instigate a bodily shut-down or something similar and, as I looked up to where we were going in the steely dawn light, I realised it was very high and that I was a very poor skier and would, somehow, have to get down the hill.

A sense of defeat and loss breezed over me. The one that comes with a hangover and the realisation that you are not up to performing any task and especially not the one in hand.

I looked back at Malcolm who was half asleep but gritting his chattering teeth as we wound our remorseless way to the top.

It was light by the time we arrived but howlingly cold and I made a hash of dismounting the lift as I always did. A less expert man than Bill would have been flattened by my shaking descent onto the landing area over his skis.

I was confused by my surroundings.

There was what looked like a sheer drop to my left and a wall of orange netting hung with signs showing a skull with the word, familiar to every British schoolboy of my age, ACHTUNG!!! to my right. I remember wondering why it wasn't in French and were they only warning German people?

Neither of these routes looked in any way accessible let alone ski-able and we were the only three people at this zenith. Chair after chair came up behind us on the wires but they were all empty.

We remained alone in the eerie half-light, and I began to worry that there was no way down.

Malcolm peered, red-eyed and nauseous, into the grey of the morning, Bill lit yet another joint and, to delay whatever was going to happen next, I engaged him in conversation much as you might the captain of your firing squad.

He was not a talented talker, and his sentences were short and without much decoration.

'Have you been up here before, Bill?' I asked.

'Yup.' He said.

'Looks very steep…both sides, they look very steep.' I said and I noticed my voice quavering a bit. Still, that might be the cold.

'Yup.' He said.

'Isn't that quite dangerous when it's so grey and things?' I asked.

'Yup.' He said.

There was a brief hiatus while he sucked his joint deep into his fetid lungs. I thought I would change tack.

'Where are you from, Bill?'

'Around.' He answered with a sigh.

'Around?' I queried.

'Yup.' He said.

'America?' I turned around to make sure Malcolm was still with us, but his gaze hadn't altered.

'Some.' He started to shuffle his skis back and forth and prised the knub of the joint from his lips and threw it down onto the snow and spat a few times.

'Have you finished nattering away?' Malcolm asked.

'Yup.' Said Bill and I, in unison.

In the silence that followed, exaggerated by the dead atmosphere and the cold, I said.

'You know I'm a very inexperienced skier, Bill? I haven't skied for ages and....''Should have said.' Bill drawled. 'Lady said yous two were real good.'I began to understand just how far Jo had taken this.

It was a perfect pay-back for our night of roistering without them. I would have seen the funny side were I not cold, feeling like death and very frightened.

Malcolm was a superb skier, I had been told, and Bill, being a guide, was obviously fine to descend, but I was faced with a ghastly, lonely end.

'Just how bad are you?' Bill asked. 'Was that falling over thing not a joke?'

'No, that's what I do.' I said, a little panic shrilling some of the words.

'Shee-it.' Said Bill.

Malcolm seemed unworried by my plight.

'It's just sliding down a mountain on snow.' He pointed out helpfully. 'We'll help you down. We'll just ski down a bit with you then wait for you and so on.' He smiled. 'We'll do it in stages.'

'Yup.' Said Bill but he didn't look very convinced.

He pointed at the netting and the skull signs.

'Be easier here.' He said pointing at the void with his stick. 'No people to worry us and deep snow.'It sounded both encouraging and discouraging depending on how you viewed the absence of people and the presence of deep snow.

'Let's give it a go.' Said Malcolm and stepped on the netting with his skis and shuffling over. Bill and I joined him. I stood beside Macolm and watched as the view banished his hangover. It looked like the scenery from the start of a spy film or a wild skiing documentary.

'What the fuck? What the fuck?' I said.

'I know, beautiful isn't it?' Malcolm said and started sliding towards what would be a point of no return.

'I'm never going to get down that.' I said pointing at the white expanse.

'Maybe, maybe not.' Said Bill helpfully.

'Well you've got to get down somehow.' Malcolm said, 'Let's just take it slow.' He said and launched himself down the hill.

'Looking good.' Said Bill and did the same.

They were soon just two dots at the bottom of the first slope.

I was left alone and quivering like an undecided suicide, when the idea suddenly passed through my mind that, if I were to reach them at the same speed, in no time at all we would be at the bottom of the hill and having breakfast in the warmth of a restaurant; croissants, hot chocolate, maybe even a café cognac and a ciggie while we laughed at this adventure.

I pushed myself off and hadn't gone five yards when I fell sideways into the deep, deep snow. I had never skied in powder snow of this depth or, indeed, of any depth and, as I struggled to get myself upright a feeling of desolation swept over me.

When, after a titanic human effort, I managed to right myself I realised I was not on the track the others had gouged for me but flailing about in my own pathway. I could see the others, mere ants in the distance below, obviously trying to locate me. I was in so deep and my entire frame so covered in snow that I must have been invisible.

I tried to bully my way through the drifts, but I was making little progress and the sweat that had now burst from my every pore from the effort was turning to ice on each part of my body that was not covered.I stopped and was about to weep when I suddenly remembered something I had heard about leaning back on your skis in deep snow.

It seemed counterintuitive, but I decided to give it a go.

By the time I had learnt that it certainly did aid progress, and very quickly at that, I had also discovered that it was impossible to turn or slow down. It was as if I was surfing over the snow and, unable to tell where I was going, I thought I should bring my vertical progress to an end and falling over sideways seemed the only option.

This just took me fast in another direction and, by the time I came to a barrelling, bone-shaking halt, I was deep under snow and the world had become dark and completely silent.

I think I did weep at this point.

I struggled out of the snow to find one ski had come off and was being held on by the safety strap that I had scoffed at, but that Bill had insisted I wore.

Despite this, it was just then that I began to develop a hatred for Bill that became so deep and all-encompassing that I knew I was going to get down just so I could kill him.

I finally caught up with them, lungs bursting, legs like jelly and sweating like a pig to be met by Bill, leaning on his poles.

'Where you bin, Jesus, have you never skied before?' He said.

Malcolm tried to be more circumspect.

'Well done, are you OK? You seemed to have a lot of....' But, before he could finish, with a little skip onto his skis, Bill was off down the mountain.

'Shit.' Said Malcolm and pushed himself off after him.

'Fuck's sake!' I cried out after them. 'Wait for me.'

But they were now again two dots halfway down the next slope which seemed to be covered in snow that was less deep and slightly more recognisable as a piste.

The grey of the day made any judgement of distance hazy but I needed to keep up with them as they were just about to go around a corner and out of my sight.

I pushed myself off from where I stood and immediately realised that the slope was considerably steeper and the snow more compact than I had guessed. Before I could properly assess my predicament, I was travelling far too fast for my limited skills and, trying to slow myself down just seemed to keep me at the same pace while losing direction so I pointed myself down the hill and allowed gravity and fate to do their work.

They did this so admirably that I arrived at the bottom of the slope going very fast, thank you gravity, and piled, headlong into a drift made up of large, hard lumps of snow that had obviously been pushed there by some sort of snowplough, thank you fate.

I was too physically exhausted and cold to feel much pain but, as I extricated myself, I could feel a few grazes on uncovered parts of my anatomy, but nothing appeared to be wrong with my limbs.

'Fuck me.' Said Malcolm and Bill in unison and,

'Are you OK?' Said Malcolm, alone.

'Not really, you arseholes, I have not skied for years and I wasn't any good then and now you....'My tirade was cut off by Bill warning us.

'We better make tracks and get on. I don't like the look of these clouds and we've got to get over the stream and onto the flat ground down there.' He pointed vaguely to his left and downwards.

'Stream? What stream?' I asked, my voice cracking.

'Just a stream we need to get over.' Bill pointed with his stick.

'Is it far?' I asked breathlessly, trying to get my skis back on my boots.

'Quite a ways but, once we're over that the next bit, it's plain sailing.'And he did his infuriating disappearing act and Malcolm followed.

I was now so thirsty that I thought I might soon be overtaken by the madness that sailors suffer when there is water, water everywhere but not a drop to drink only, in this case snow, snow, everywhere.

I tried to remember what the right thing to do was, regarding snow. Could you eat it or not? Did it send you mad, like salt water, or could you suck on a lump and let it thaw to water on your tongue?

I tried some of the fluffier type but a mouthful barely converted into a spoonful of water and a lump of iced snow froze my tongue and my lips and, frankly, made me begin to cry a bit.

I took a deep breath, pulled myself together, spat out the icy lump and turned to slide around the corner.

About two hundred yards down the path, there was a small collection of people, which included Bill and Malcolm, surrounding what was obviously an 'incident'.

There were some regular skiers and a couple of orange-clad people with some contraption or other and they were leaning over and looking down.

In no time at all I was among them, literally as I had arrived too quickly and my attempt to stop with a little jiggle of my hips had gone awry and I took one of the orange man's legs from under him.

As we all shuffled back to our feet, I saw the problem. To the side of the path, which thinned to a maximum of two skis width, and down a very steep bank of about twenty feet, there was a hole in the snow from which a lady's head projected, under which was a fast-moving stream in which stood most of the rest of this poor woman.

All of us were packed onto the last piece of flat snow after which the skinny path started and to the left of the cavity at the bottom of which lay the watery hole.

If this were a book about an Arctic expedition written in the 1900s, there would be a pen and ink drawing explaining this scenario with A's and B's marking each salient point of reference.

But it is not, so you will have to take my word for it.

My first question was, obviously,

'Does anyone have any water?' to which I didn't receive an answer as everyone seemed too preoccupied with the lady in the stream. I approached one of the men from what had now become apparent, was the skiing version of the St John Ambulance Brigade.

'*De l'eau, Monsieur, avez vous de l'eau?*' I asked the taller of the two who pointed at the raging stream.

'*Non, Monsieur, pour de boire, pour moi.*' I mimed drinking a glass of water. It seemed odd for these gnarled, rescue chaps not to have any water.

'*Non.*' The one I had asked answered firmly and looked away, then looked back at me and added firmly, ' *Et je suis une femme.*'

'*Ah, bien sur, mais oui, pardonnez-moi, Mademoiselle.*' I burbled as she fixed me with a beady stare.

'*Madame.*' She added gruffly and turned back to the job in hand.

The two of them had erected a sort of pully system with climbing ropes and pitons and it was very impressive.

They managed, with some difficulty, but remarkable calm, to pull the lady out of the stream, who was unsurprisingly crying with fear and relief. They took off her skis, wrapped her, packed her and got her over the ravine with a sort of bridge contraption and, in what seemed like just a few minutes, were standing on the other side with the lady as snug as a bug on a sledge.

I was extremely impressed and said so and was about to ask if I could use their bridge when I saw the look in the eyes of the lady paramedic I'd offended and decided not to.

She pulled on a rope and the whole doings collapsed into a mess of rope and metal which she hauled up and whipped into a coil which she put in a rucksack and scooped over her shoulder. Then, with one last, bitter look at me, she and her partner shot off down the hill, pulling the stretcher.

Silence fell.

I stared, terrified and without hope, at the pathway across the crevasse and then started to berate Bill as an irresponsible, thoughtless, dangerous piece of excrescence that would only be found on the shoe of a..... you get my drift.

So hot, thirsty, angry and apprehensive was I that my tirade shocked even Bill who was stoned to the point of mental numbness.

'How the fuck am I meant to get back?' I screamed at him.

The real question was 'how are we all going to get back' but my state had rendered me selfish to the extreme.

'Like this.' Bill said and executed an unbelievably neat little *schuss* down the short slope, squatted and pushed himself off his ski-sticks up the opposite slope, straightened his back towards the top and then stretched upwards the way ski jumpers do and landed softly on the flat surface beyond the small valley.

It was very impressive, beautifully executed and very annoying. As I began to call out,

'Yes, but what the fuck am I meant to do?' But he was gone as fast as his skis could carry him.

'You bastard, you arsehole, you....' I screamed after him but It was futile and I was anyway near the point of collapse.

The other two people, friends of the saved woman, were obviously extremely proficient skiers otherwise they would never have been on this insane part of the mountain and, although not with Bill's grace and elan, they negotiated the valley in a risk free and workmanlike way.

They then, very nobly, stood on the other side to make sure I got over, unlike the little rat Bill.

This turned out to be just as well.

Malcolm explained to me what to do but it meant very little.

I pushed myself off the top and tried to squat and thrust myself up the other side but mistimed my squat and ended up having no impetus and so was consigned to the nadir of the valley on a foot-wide path with the freezing, raging torrent below.

My skis were forming a bridge across the bottom of this scoop and I was as incapacitated as a beetle on its back.

There was much discussion about my situation, and nobody would be able to pass unless I moved. The safest method appeared to be for the people on the other side to send down a sleeve of an anorak for me to hold onto and gradually release myself from the angle and then for them to haul me up. This took a very long time indeed but, after several unnerving slides towards nemesis, I got to the other side.

The relief was overpowering and, for the second time that morning, I toyed with blubbing.

Now it was only left for Malcolm to make it over and he employed the fast approach method but, not being as agile as Bill he mistimed his run but we just caught his proffered stick and managed to pull him to safety.

I thanked the lovely couple who had stayed and adjusted my bandana up from where it had slipped over my nose. They returned my thanks with a look that a grown-up might give to a child who they knew was the object of abusive parents but couldn't see how best to intervene.

I think it was my tweed britches that elicited the sympathy.

I took a deep breath and pulled up my socks, literally and made sure my kit was all in place for what I had been promised was the gentle *schuss* home. Malcolm and I shuffled to the corner of the path and looked around the base of the mountain.

There, as far as the eye could see, were skiers who had descended from every slope around, pushing themselves, struggling uphill on a far from flat incline to a pub of some sort at the bottom of a set of ski lifts.

I could spot Bill in the distance and began to howl abuse at him as loudly as my parched throat and bursting blood vessels allowed.

Many of the skiers turned around to see what sort of beast might have made such a noise.

I was going to kill him when I caught up with him and had convinced myself that a life of incarceration in a Swiss jail wouldn't be so bad and certainly worth the price of watching Bill bleed out in the snow.

I began the slow, muscle-burning *langlauf* up the slope to the bar, maddened by thirst and sobbing with hatred for Bill and everything to do with winter sports. It seemed to take for ever and I was passed by many people of all ages who seemed to be snow-skating up the hill with ease, pushing themselves nimbly off their ski-sticks.

As the bar got nearer, I began to imagine the cooling drinks I was going to order, and they appeared before me in shimmering mirages.

When, at last, I found myself outside the bar, I shook off my skis and threw them with my sticks onto the flat snow. I was making simpering noises that attracted some sympathetic people to ask after my health.

'You need to stand those up.' A strident English voice admonished me.

'Wha?' I croaked back.

'Stand those up with your poles attached so they don't get in people's way and so you don't lose them.' It continued.

'Wha?' I asked again but I was too tired to argue and fulfilled this little, sensible duty and clumped onto the floor of the outdoor bar.

This was a sort of wooden decking strewn with lumps of hard snow forming a large terrace covered with tables all packed with people lounging about sipping drinks, eating, smoking and smiling.

I was about to join them, and a little happiness seeped back into my jaded body and mind.

I turned around to find a mass of people queuing for service and realised I was going to have to wait a very long time so, to my shame, I began to bully my way to the front of the crowd, growling out reasons and excuses for my barbaric and selfish behaviour, when I saw Bill at the front of the queue.

I exploded.

'You miserable arsehole, you rat, you piece of filth…' and so I went on, barging through these poor people until I was by his side at the front of the mass of civilised people quietly waiting their turn.

There is no doubt that, for a moment, I became unhinged.

Bill cowered, as did everyone around me.

'What the fuck, man, wooah! What are you doing? What's wrong?' His voice quivered.

'What's fucking wrong…' I had meant to say but it just came out as a strange and dreadful noise.

'You left me to die!' I shouted and this did come out with crystal and dramatic clarity.

The hubbub on the deck and in the queue stopped and people shuffled around to see what was going on.

I had started as a violent and unwelcome gate crasher at this beautiful holiday scene but my shouted accusation seemed to have given me licence because the tide turned and Bill was now the villain and he realised it.

'Sorry mate.' He said, 'I truly didn't know you were such a pathetic skier. Jo told me you were world class.'

In a second, my wrath turned to Jo. It was her that had set this up to get her own back for my keeping Malcolm out all night. My anger with Bill began to abate but did not decrease, just found a new direction.

'Aha!' I said like someone in a Victorian melodrama, 'Aha!' I said again for good measure.

The crowd realised that some sort of rapprochement had been reached and the hubbub resumed. I was also at the front of the queue.

'Can I get you a drink, mate?' Bill asked.

'I would like four Coca Colas and a bottle of water.' I said for no real reason other than I remained slightly unhinged.

Bill handed me these on a tray and fled the scene. There was no sign of Malcolm, but we had all agreed to meet there.

I took the tray, unable to drink while my hands were already engaged, and elbowed my belligerent way towards the edge of the deck where I felt I could at least lean on the fence and drink.

I had gone no more than three paces when I stepped onto a patch of ice, my boots shot into the air and I fell, horizontal, onto the hard wood decking. Not only was this extremely painful but the drinks tumbled from the tray and fell with a terrible crash, covering me in foaming Coke as lumps of ice shot everywhere and the glasses splintered into scattering shards.

I shouted garbled obscenities as I watched all the precious liquid hit the ground, spending itself into the cracks between the planks. I scrabbled around gesticulating and wailing in my own world of tortured thirst and complete incomprehension as to how a morning could have gone so horribly awry.

I licked any liquid I could find off the floor and rolled into a sitting position with my head between my legs. The diners had backed away, giving me a wide berth. My original, shocking behaviour had been exacerbated by this new outrage and I felt deeply embarrassed.

I stood up and stole a bottle of fizzy water from the nearest table, put my hand into my pocket, took out a note and put it on the table, only too late realizing that it was far too much money but I felt unable to ask for change, so I just strode away.

I saw Louise sitting at a table by the railings watching me and realised that, as the crowd had dispersed, she might have witnessed at least the end of my deplorable performance.

I wandered over with a thin smile.

She looked changed somehow.

'So, it was you.' She said.

'What was?' I replied as innocently as I could.

'All that kerfuffle.'

'What kerfuffle?'And so on until she said.

'The mad shouting and screaming and pushing and shoving.'

I looked mournfully down at my boots.

'Might have been.' I offered.

'And the pratfall and the desperate behaviour on the floor...'

'Probably.'

'And the swearing at people who had done nothing wrong...the drink stealing and queue barging....'

'I'm afraid so.'

We sat in silence while she let it sink into my fevered mind just how dreadful this episode must have seemed.

'I've had a terrible morning.' I said 'I might have died.'

'So have I.' Louise said and added. 'And so might I have done.'This was annoying because it was a) perfect grammar and b) diluted my story.

I felt, in the light of my embarrassing performance I should let her go first.

'Why, what happened?' I asked, hoping it was a quick story so I could get to mine as soon as possible.

It wasn't.

She had endured the most terrible morning, having been abandoned by the class she was skiing with outside a cable car stop, and found herself on a precipitous and icy black run that came down under the funicular and between the pylons that held the cables up.

She had been terrified and cold and could only slide down this sheer slope as best she could, hanging on to anything that might slow her descent while experienced skiers raced past her, not one of them stopping until she had arrived, bruised and freezing at the foot of the run.

I told her my story and we stared into space for a while like two members of the crew newly returned from the *Endeavour*.

Most of the people who had witnessed my meltdown had left, so I was no longer the subject of lingering stares.

There was no sign of Malcolm or Jo whom we both blamed for our hideous mornings.

We discussed just how pointless we found the sport; how hideous the clothes were and how gaudy and overpriced the kit.

We agreed that everyone was rude and pushy and that we were unlikely to find anyone we would want to hang out with on the slopes. We agreed that the pistes had been taken over by the froggy bottom of humanity and that we would never come anywhere near the Alps again.

But, most of all, we accepted that we were both hopeless skiers and we didn't like being cold or tired.

This cheered us up immensely, so we drank a lot of different, comical drinks, some warm and some cold, left our skis outside the bar and lurched back to our chalet in the happy knowledge that neither of us would ever go skiing again.

18

A Tailor's Dummy

I have been lucky enough, in a somewhat chaotic life, to have known some wonderful people. Those whose kindness and generosity has touched me and helped me no end and others who have made me laugh more than I ever thought possible; people whose mentorship and advice was faultless but never taken and those whose love, nearly always returned, has lifted life to the wonder it is.

I have met and befriended, spent occasional minutes and sometimes years with, some extraordinary people, sometimes world famous but far more often unknown. Geniuses, artists, musicians, writers, a throbbing universe of brilliant and companionable people some of whom have had the glittering prizes heaped on them and many more whose talents the world, and often their closest friends, have yet to appreciate.

Some of them are rich, but mostly not, some are eccentric, but all are marvellous company and originals but, to a person, they add to the enjoyment of the haphazard wonder of life.

I have always been drawn to imaginative souls and find them and those with little regard for money far more enjoyable company.

I have also been unbelievably fortunate in my wife and children, who mean more to me than I could possibly express.

They, and my friends have all been exceptionally long suffering towards me for little in return except the occasional laugh.

Amongst this rackety jumble of humanity, some have stood out for their very individuality and the way they have approached life widdershins.

Some of these benign outlaws were dear friends and some I met only rarely but each of them brightened up my and many other people's lives.

One of these came in the extraordinary figure of Enrico, Baron di Portanova, Ricky to his many friends.

His provenance was much discussed, and nobody seemed to share the same story. He was said to have been born in Los Angeles, Texas or Naples on an uncertain date but generally agreed to be 1926 though Ricky claimed it was 1933 to shave a few years off his age and make any investigation into his background that bit more difficult.

His father was an Italian playboy called Paolo Apruzzo who caught the eye of a Miss Cullen, the daughter of one of America's richest men and a wildcat oilman. The origin of Ricky's Barony was also shrouded in mystery and his father opined, 'I must be the only man who has inherited a title from his son.'

Paolo and Lillie Cullen married in due course and, rather embarrassingly soon for a very conservative family, begat Ricky and later his brother Ugo who never really featured in the legend.

The young Apruzzo family lived a reasonably privileged life in LA but they soon divorced and his mother moved to New York while Ricky and his brother moved back to Italy with their priapic father.

After much carousing as a young man and a marriage to a Yugoslavian athlete, his grandfather died and Ricky suddenly found himself the recipient of a $5k per month stipend, a goodly sum in the 1960s.

His father, however, realised that this was actually absurdly little given that his son was the oldest surviving child and kicked up a stink so successfully that Ricky became hugely rich.

I was never really aware of this backstory when first I met him but, as he was such a comical figure and many of his intimates were equally so, I chose to believe both all and none of the myths surrounding him. He had married Sandra, a local Texan woman from quite humble origins, who was enormous fun, highly intelligent, sexy and curvy, indeed, she was probably the reason he lived as long as he did, even to seventy though no-one could be quite sure.

She did what she could to control this extraordinary specimen through his raging alcoholism, bad behaviour, relentless spending and debauchery though, surprisingly, he was an outstandingly kind man and, when the bottle didn't interfere, a fascinating raconteur if even half of his stories were true.

Visually he was a confusing treat for a connoisseur of humanity. Although hardly in middle age when I first met him, his face had the somewhat ravaged remains of a matinee idol with a shining tan, highlighted by some Trumpian make-up. He had a swirling black toupee and a very thin pencil moustache that a stage cad might have worn to out-rotter even Terry-Thomas.

It was a fabulously individual look, made even more so by his wig which, for some reason, was appallingly badly made so it slipped around his head often and generously. When drunk, which was most of the time, this could hide a large part of his face while he continued to converse in a serious way in his rich baritone about whatever theory had recently caught his fancy.

His deep, mellifluous voice had been honed while he was a voice-over artist for films in Rome during its *Dolce Vita* period, dubbing Italian into English and vice versa. His accent and delivery were hugely theatrical, as if he were continuously declaiming Shakespearean lines, and his accent was a sort of grand and courtly English with a transatlantic twang.

As I hadn't known him during his rise to vast riches and the lifestyle he came to inhabit, I had to judge his and Sandra's lives as

I found them which was so sumptuous, preposterous and unlike anything I, and many people far more louche and worldly than me, had ever seen that, in trying to describe it, I feel like a delivery boy might sound and returning from Xanadu and being asked by his boss what it was like.

He had been a jeweller at some stage in Rome and Sandra was always covered in enormous, bright gems and I even made the occasional commissioned piece for them.

He had the most operatic of Italian taste allied to Texan ostentation so there was absolutely nothing timid or understated about Ricky or, indeed, Sandra.

He lived, when in London for the season, in a permanent suite at Claridge's but his proclivity for relieving himself informally in unexpected places, like the corner of rooms or in a lift, became too much for the management.

It was said that he had come across a young couple who were enjoying the first night of their marriage in the hotel dining room, and he congratulated them while peeing into their ice bucket. This was considered *de trop* and he was finally banned.

He had lived in Monte Carlo when he was first rich, and the South of France remained his summer base. When not travelling or in Texas he lived in a house outside Acapulco in Mexico that was absurdly over the top by any yardstick.

It was called The Villa Arabesque and it was built into a cliff face going down to the sea.

The main house was a warren of extraordinary and voluminous spaces that included an entire room for wrapping presents, an everyday feature of their life, a discotheque and their enormous bedroom topped off by a huge open terrace above. Much of the day was spent on a vast open space covered with strange statues which led to three abstractly shaped swimming pools.

The nine spare rooms were all lavishly themed and, hewn out of the side of a cliff as they were, had to be reached by a funicular that crawled up the side of the rock face from the private beach bellow. When they were in residence, the whole estate was in permanent party mode and wildly eccentric like the host.

It was once used, without any changes having to be made, as a set for a James Bond film.

His average day was baffling and Ricky, if not caught before the effects of drink had begun to tell, was difficult to converse with. Although we met often and I had both been to many of his parties and actually made jewellery for him, he got into his mind that I was a classically trained theatre actor performing the great roles he had so craved himself as a young man.

After some years of trying to disavow him, I followed Sandra's lead by giving up trying to explain to him that I was the same person he had sat down with, only days before, in my studio.

This sometimes became awkward as he would come up to me at parties and boom,

'What are you giving London at the moment, The Bard? Sheridan, Shaw, pray tell.'

'You know Theo, of course? Oh, to be young and treading the boards as he does.'

Friends came to understand what was happening but for some time I bumped into strangers to whom he had introduced me who asked what I was 'in at the moment'.

The added bonus of acquaintanceship with Ricky was being introduced to some of his more outlandish friends. Although many of his wide circle were rich Texans, showbiz people or cafe society he had some spectacularly disparate contacts of no discernible background or nationality, and some seemed to have hailed from operetta states or Marx Brothers principalities.

One, who I shall call Benito, was the cultural attaché to Mexico from a state none of us had heard of, although he was actually Mexican himself. This diplomatic post allowed him to behave almost as he wished, pay no taxes and park his car, decorated with a magnificently grand badge, flag and mascot, anywhere in any Mexican town.

The best part for him, I am sure, was that, as the Portanovas most often dressed for dinner, he was able to wear his splendidly extravagant and theatrical diplomatic uniform.

I am certain that he designed this himself.

It held a riot of orders and sashes, medals and ribbons which covered his small chest, for he was a slight man, and a plumed hat that he would keep on while we had drinks until, at the very last moment that we sat down to dinner, he would take it off with a magnificent flourish.

Neither his hosts, nor the many other invited and self-invented people that formed their milieu, ever questioned the provenance of the uniform or the medals as no one ever questions anyone's life story in that famously opaque country. His every move and sentence, called out in a high and operatic talking voice, used to make me howl with laughter but he was taken very seriously by most of the guests as, indeed, he was by himself.

Ricky's chosen daytime outfits in Mexico or in any sunny clime were Safari suits made by the great Horacio.

I know the name of his tailor because I went there once to be fitted for similar outfits. I was taken by Leslie Bricusse, a very old and dear friend who had a house near Acapulco and habitually wore these outfits whenever and wherever it was warm enough. Lesley travelled with just a few of these and never looked eccentric in them as he had made the look his own. He had black and darker coloured ones for the evening and a host of pastel colours for the day which he teamed with a couple of pairs of butter-soft moccasins.

It seemed to me a very sophisticated way to travel with three or four changes of outfits, all packed into a small briefcase.

Unfortunately, when I went to see the great tailor with Leslie, we had enjoyed rather a long lunch and an ambition to be clothed forever in different versions of safari suits had taken hold of me.

Leslie was no help as he encouraged me to ever more absurd flights of sartorial fancy.

It became obvious that each of his customers had their own individual safari suit quirk and that these unique vanities were extremely important to Horacio. Leslie had special flaps over a multitude of pockets and Ricky had his suits made with special inserts built for his cigarillos to poke out of, rather like a *bandido* might have had for bullets. It was his very personal affectation and it suited him.

When the great man asked me, very gravely, what I wanted as my signature eccentricity, I was stumped. Eventually, when pressed, I said that I would like the sleeves slightly longer than was usual and the trousers slightly tighter.

I should have heeded Horacio's raised eyebrow.

I chose three 'silks', a slubbed orange, a plain scarlet and a black material with dragons picked out in a sort of jacquard. Even Leslie was taken aback but, nearing the slightly tetchy stage where the end of a jolly lunch meets the beginnings of an early evening hangover, I persisted petulantly.

The cotton colours I chose were slightly more practical. These were were off-white, a very pale strawberry pink and, of course khaki. For the last of these I gave endless instructions as I wanted it to be as near as possible to a genuine safari suit with belts and pleated pockets all over the place.

I had seen *Born Free* and knew the details intimately.

Exhausted, we returned to Leslie's house where we made free with the tequila.

I had forgotten all about these suits until a very neat box containing these beauties appeared only minutes before we left for the airport. I decanted them into my case and I was proved right, six of them hardly took up any room. However, I had been rather alarmed by the flashes of colour as I unpacked and re-packed them.

We arrived back to London on a rather grey, depressing day and made our way home. As I began to unload my suitcases, the new suiting was at the top of my case.

I took out the first suit, which happened to be the one in scarlet silk, and Louise fell silent.

'What do you think?' I asked somewhat nervously as it was neither the colour nor the material I had remembered.

'What is it?' She answered, genuinely baffled.

'A safari suit like Leslie's and Ricky's.' I tried.

'No it isn't.' she said 'It's nothing like theirs, it's red and made of some terrible material.'

'Silk.' I said.

'No it isn't.' She came over and rubbed the shirt between her thumb and finger.

'Silk.' I said again.

'Nope.' She shook her head. 'It's something horrible.'

'Silk.' I repeated. 'You don't think Horacio would use some sort of polyester when he's made these suits for so many famous and discerning people, do you?'

'Yup.'

'I shall try it on.' I said boldly.

'You do that.' She smirked and so I undressed to my underpants.

There was obviously a reason that the Mexican *modiste* cut all his trousers the same way.

The main point of non-action safari suits is their comfort and looseness in tropical climes. The oppressive tightness of the trousers I had requested, only as a sop to Horacio's wish that every client had their own unique point of difference, turned out not to have been a good idea. I had noticed the fine artisan cock an eyebrow at this choice and now I knew why.

They were meant to fit like only slightly more tailored pyjama bottoms, but these were cut so boldly that even that stalwart of the skin-tight trouser, Rod Stewart, might have wept.

I struggled to get them over my knees and then they snagged on my thighs.

Ricky, as I have mentioned, wore safari suits during the day with his cigars aggressively displayed twinned with various sandals of unusual ethnicity. He wore a bejewelled ring or two, one of which was decorated with his fantastical coat of arms, and one or two bracelets.

I began to consider the difference in my lifestyle and living conditions to both Leslie and Ricky. They were older, rich and had no job that required any sort of practical clothing and, more importantly, they spent most of their time in blazing sunshine.

I gave up on the red one but, as we were going to drinks at a friend's house that evening in a brave attempt to stay up through jet lag, I decided to wear the pinkish linen one to test the water, so to speak.

Somehow it didn't look as natural on me as it did on both Ricky and Leslie, who seemed to inhabit theirs like second skins. I looked as if I was wearing some sort of vaguely institutional protective clothing.

Neither did my requested length of sleeve work as it suggested I had some malformation of the arms. The tightness of the trousers was uncomfortable to say the least and they clung to both my thighs and calves. Disappointingly, there was nothing to suggest these could possibly have been tailored for me, at some expense, and by the king of the safari suit himself.

Worse was to come when we walkedout into a South London, overcast March evening and I found myself frozen to the bone. I was ill at ease in every way but I was determined to carry on as I believed that I could get used to wearing them and my friends might become accustomed to seeing me in them.

Louise stifled a laugh as we made our way to the car but I wasn't going to be put off.

After she had parked - and I still believe further away from the party than was necessary - we had quite a distance to walk along reasonably busy pavements. I have rarely caused such a reaction, even in drag or ridiculous fancy dress, as I did in the pink safari suit.

It seemed an inexplicable outfit and appeared to baffle people as they continued to stare at me well after I had passed them. I still have no real understanding of why this humble bolt of pink linen engendered such a reaction.

When we arrived at the party conversation almost stopped and an old friend of mine, Henry, famously laconic and dry, sauntered over and said,

'What on earth are you wearing? You've gone far too far this time.'

'It's a safari suit.' I answered.

'What are you hoping to bag down here, then?' He asked. 'Squirrels? Moles?' he added.

'It's not actually for a safari, Henry, it's a way to dress less formally, more a lifestyle choice.' I answered with as much condescension as I could muster.

'Ah, is that so?' He replied languidly. 'And just when did you decide your future lay in California, as the dentist in residence for a disturbing sex cult?'

Comments throughout the evening followed in this tone and I was shaken by people's reaction to such a mild divergence from the norm. I had worn far more bizarre outfits which garnered little or no comment at all.

But, there was no doubt that the first safari suit had failed its test and I was to find that, one by one the others did too.

The red one, for some reason, was tighter than the others and I never managed to get either the shirt or trousers on and, as Louise had maintained, as it was not silk it ended its days rubbing down the windscreen.

The white one, which made me look as if I was about to perform a complicated plastic surgery procedure, was befouled on its first outing by misplaced spaghetti bolognese which proved impossible to remove.

The black one made me look like a Viet Cong pimp who had recently been found hiding from a war he thought was still raging around him. What's more, by the end of its only wearing, it smelt like an overused canal.

The orange one I also wore just once.

It was in the South of France on a balmy evening.

Sitting on a sofa, looking like a giant tangerine and enjoying a drink before dinner, I found an ancient and brilliant English film director's hand on my thigh.

'Orange is one of my turn ons,' He whispered. 'And you wear it so well.'

I was caught in many minds but my admiration for his work, a perverse thrill at being chatted up in early middle age by anyone at all and his being the first person to have liked any of my suits were obvious plusses.

Conversely the knowledge that someone, of whatever sex or proclivity, could be excited by a person wearing orange polyester outweighed the positives.

Last was the khaki safari suit.

This was the only one I'd not had the trousers tightened or the sleeves shortened on and so it was a classic, timeless number. It had lots of flap pockets and a belt; it was original and flawless.

I first wore it to travel to the Isle of Wight to stay with some friends for a bank holiday weekend.

There was a mood, I could tell, amongst my family that this might be an inappropriate outfit for a drive through the home counties, but I pointed out how comfortable it was and how practical.

As we approached the ferry, the traffic came to a standstill, and we queued to drive onto the boat. After ten minutes or so and bored, I got out of the car and stood on the bottom of the car's doorway to allow me the extra height to see how long the line was. As I put my hand up over my eyebrows to shield my view from the sun, I looked out over the ocean as had so many travellers before me.

'Oi!' shouted a raucous voice. 'Oi, you!'

I turned around to see a man in shorts and a string vest which imprisoned his vast and pendulous gut, standing with his hands on his hips, some three or four cars behind us.

I cocked a quizzical eyebrow at him.

'Yeah, you, Dr fuckin' Livingstone.' He shouted out.

People began to get out of their cars their interest piqued by something happening in the boredom of the queue.

'Can I help?' I asked.

'You're in the wrong fuckin' queue.' He said.

I looked around to see if there were any signs for another line but could see none.

'How do you mean?' I asked politely.

He pointed into the distance, over to my left.

'Africa's that way, mate.' He said and the whole crowd of waiting travellers began to laugh and jeer.

Safari suits are for safaris.

19

A Diplomatic Incident

Many years ago, Louise and I were asked to a very smart embassy dinner for a South American nation that had recently re-joined the democratic world after an experiment with totalitarianism.

To this day we have no idea why we were invited.

We only knew one other couple and they had a very good reason to be there.

The invitation stipulated black tie, but we arrived to find many of the guests in exotic uniforms with many ribbons, medals and sparkling orders slung around their chests of the sort you would expect on the South American diplomats who made up the majority of the guests.

There was a small smattering of well-known Brits from the arts and a few politicians and, I dare say, foreign diplomats who we would not have recognised.

I was amazed by the grandeur and extravagance of the interior of what was the embassy for a fairly impoverished nation. The furniture, pictures and silver were extraordinarily lavish, and there was a small army of liveried staff. It seemed embarrassingly grand, in fact, given that the vast majority of the population it represented were so famously poor.

It always seems contrary to good diplomacy to ask the world for financial help to stem the rising tide of poverty in your native country when the request comes from an urban palace in the heart of Kensington.

We met the ambassador and his wife, who were both extremely nattily dressed, at the door and a flunkey boomed out our names.

We exchanged pleasantries before moving on into a general milling around in a large reception room.

These sorts of things are always awkward when you are presented with a sea of unfamiliar faces and, exacerbated in this case, by trying to keep any sort of diplomatic straight face surrounded by so many guests dressed as *opéra bouffe* sovereigns.

We murmured to each other and Louise, who is far more skilled at approaching strangers, smiled at marooned couples and made conversation with others, bringing me into the conversation once she had tested the water.

It is for this sort of affair that the art of 'exchanging pleasantries' is refined by diplomats..

We were called into dinner where the grandeur of the table was extraordinary, laden with huge pieces of silver, an array of knives and forks and a sea of glasses that would have put Bacchus to shame.

I sat between two very jolly ladies and had those sorts of conversations, first with one and then the other and then back again as the courses came and went, that followed the tried and tested subjects at any dinner where the guests aren't their hosts' actual friends.

When guests have been chosen, perhaps for their beneficence, amusement value or usefulness, their social standing, fame or usefulness, as at this sort of dinner, it is always unnerving when you realise you don't possess any of the attributes that the hosts were hoping for.

Once your neighbours have discovered this and have given up trying to work out why you are there, they tend to spend more time speaking with the people on the other side of them.

However charming and witty you try to be, or can be, once the smile of confidence disappears to be replaced by that shy rictus, you are on a turning wicket.

It turned out that the main reasons for the dinner were for the Ambassador to make a long speech and then introduce a compatriot, a wine maker, who also gave us a long speech in halting English on the stupendous quality of his produce.

The reason for the profusion of wine-glasses in front of each guest became clear and was to allow us to try each of the wines he was touting.

Neither Louise nor I still drank then so I could only surmise that we had been asked to this glorified wine tasting on my past form in that direction and that whoever had done the research had failed to discover that I had become teetotal. Looking around the table, halfway through the tasting, I could see that the bulk of their analysis had been more reliable and there were some very ruddy faces.

After the endless fountain of wine, there were neither liqueurs nor port so we returned to mill about in the room we had milled in before to be given coffee.

Standing up while milling always makes managing coffee awkward, especially having to make yourself part of a knot of standing talkers. This normally involves insinuating your body into the group with eyebrow and head movements while burning your lips on the coffee.

Suddenly, from behind me, there was the unmistakable noise of slipping claws as two huge Great Danes came into the room and caused little pockets of havoc as they bumped into the guests. As this diversion died down and the dogs seemed to disappear, I realised the conversation around me was in Spanish and the group was waiting for my answer to a question. I had to shrug and, as soon as they lost interest, I sidled away.

I looked for Louise and couldn't see her she but there was another group speaking English and looking down at the floor where there was what seemed to be a pool of steaming liquid.

I assumed it was coffee so I said, by way of an opening gambit, 'Bad luck.'

'Don't know what it is.' Said one of them in heavily accented English as I caught sight of Louise coming over from one of the doors with a broad grin and holding up her very damp velvet skirt.

'Accident?' I asked.

'You'll never guess what's just happened.' She said to the assembled grandees.

Without waiting for an answer, she went straight into her tale.

'Did you see those enormous dogs?' She asked and we all nodded.

'Well, they're the Ambassador's. He has no children and he absolutely dotes on them.' We remained listening with our coffee cups poised in mid-air. Louise's ebullience had rather wrong-footed the audience.

'I was just talking to that man when I suddenly had a feeling like a hose squirting hot liquid onto my thigh and one of those huge dogs was peeing all over me. God, it was like a donkey, I was absolutely soaked so I've had to go and dry myself off in the loo.' As an afterthought she pointed at the wet, steaming floor.

I looked at the group who had heard Louise's story and thought how very differently our English friends would have reacted to this fabulously humiliating mishap. This crowd seemed concerned on her behalf but also somewhat disgusted and completely astounded that she would re-join the party drenched in dog pee and tell the story.

There was not a smile, so I thought I better lighten the mood.

'She always blames the dog when this happens.' I said with a long-suffering shrug.

They turned their backs on us and shuffled off muttering in some South America language occasionally looking back over their shoulders with distaste.

Louise hit me with her wet handbag as we got into the car.

Later, we agreed that we were a sad loss to the diplomatic corps.

20

THE WRONG BOX

When my mother died, it was her wish that she should be cremated and then buried in her family's plot in a churchyard in Staffordshire. This was a better option for all concerned than another plot in Eniskillen, but only just.

It meant she could be by her mother and father and other dead relatives but was a long way away from where the remains of her family live, bar a distant cousin or two.

Some weeks after her cremation, on the day of the internment, my sisters and I and a few others arrived at the church for a brief internment service. There are some very moving windows in the church dedicated to various short-lived cousins and uncles of hers who died in various far-flung campaigns, some plaques to long-lived academics and clerics on the walls and many and various tombstones to others of her family who no longer walk among us.

It was a grey, damp day when we arrived and we had all travelled a long way for what was, effectively, her second funeral.

The drizzle had made small pools among the graves and the ink on the order of her service, Xeroxed by a church helper, had run so badly as to make them indecipherable.

We walked behind the church towards her plot and there, yawning in the ground, was a hole that had been dug for a full-sized coffin.

The vicar looked at us approaching, his hair already matted against his head by the rain, and then turned to peer at the grave, in which stood a befuddled looking young man, leaning on a spade.

Above the hole, and also leaning on a spade, was obviously the village sexton, whose underling the boy in the hole must have been.

The vicar mouthed some platitudes in my direction and looked quizzically at the small casket which bore the ashes of my mother that I was trying to protect from the rain.

He then cocked his head, confused, but made a gesture towards the youth in the grave who was by now sitting on the edge of the grave with his feet dangling therein.

As I approached him, he slid back down to the bottom of the pit and thrust his spade into the ground so it stood up in the mud. I could now see into the hole and the pool of water that had collected on its bottom.

As I took the casket from under my coat and offered it to the young man, the sexton leant over towards it so that they formed a still and gothic Rosencrantz and Guildenstern tableau.

Had I had a skull in my hand, rather than a small box, I might have been The Dane himself.

As the two of them inspected the casket, the vicar also leaned forward as it had become obvious that we had a situation and its resolution would need some tact.

I handed the small container, no bigger than a shoe-box, to the young gravedigger. He took it solemnly into his huge hands and gazed at it. Then he looked up at me and asked,

'Is this yer Mam?'
'Yes.' I answered.

He looked dolefully at the wet casket and looked up at me, rain dripping down his blank face and said, in a bemused voice.

'She were very small when she died, weren't she?'

There was a brief hiatus before what those of the family there started to hiss and burst with laughter.

The vicar and sexton, being professional interment operators and funeral goers remained stony-faced but the young, simple lad mercifully took our reaction as the better option and started to laugh uproariously.

Among this farcical scene, the vicar said some apt words which we were unable to follow as the orders of service for the internment now looked like a very minimalist Japanese drawing.

We thanked the vicar and asked him if he would like to join us in the pub but he obviously now disapproved of us. Even telling him that one of our great uncles had been the rector at his church before the war didn't sway him and he declined.

We repaired to the pub, not expecting to reappear at the graveyard until the next one of us died and toasted a very entertaining burial.

A few months later I was in my studio when someone buzzed me to say that my cousin was in the shop.

'Which one?' I asked.

'She's got boots on' was the answer.

This narrowed it down to females, but the boots didn't really help.

I walked in to see a woman in full country, mucking-out kit with wild red hair going to grey flowing behind her like Boadicea.

This was indeed my cousin who I had not seen for some years and whose entire life had been spent amongst horses. I approached her in a familial way but as I got nearer I sensed she was in no mood for a small family gathering.

'You've put your mother in my hole.' She said loudly and aggressively, leaving me and any others in hearing distance wondering if we had heard correctly.

'I'm sorry?' I replied.

'Your mother. She's where I'm going.' She continued, 'You've buried your mother in my plot.'

'I've what?'

'Your mother is buried where I'm meant to be going.' She explained.

We had a brief conversation about how she wanted to be buried at the foot of her parents and that would entail moving my mother to the foot of *her* parents and, so intransigent was she, that I realised I was going to have to organise this move of just a few feet.

What I hadn't understood were the unbelievable complexities of doing this. It entailed involving the parish church itself and its wider, local master, the Church of England commissioners and the Home Office.

I hadn't imagined the problems accociated with disinterring a coffin, even if it only contained ashes.

After an endless and Kafkaesque series of letters, calls and conversation and not a little cost, we were ready to rebury my mother.

It was a very short affair and the pit this time was more apt for the small coffin. The headstone had already been moved and her former resting place tactfully turfed and patted down.

I left the churchyard again, assuming that now my mother really would rest in peace.

Not long after this I was contacted by a friend who lived, coincidentally, in the big house opposite the graveyard. He was a Roman Catholic but involved in and responsible for local matters as the resident nob.

He has a highly developed sense of humour and loves a jape.

'I know you had to dig your mother up and rebury her.' He said.

'Yup.' I said sensing, with some foreboding, the tone of his voice, part sympathetic and part wryly humorous.

'I may have some bad news for you.' He continued, wry humour edging sympathy into second place.

'You know what I mean by HS2, the railway line they're building?' He said, by now barely concealing his glee.

Hmm...' I said.

'Well, it's going straight through the churchyard where your Ma is buried. Looks like you'll have to dig her up again.' He finished, now not concealing his glee at all.

'Is there any room on your lawn?' I asked.

Mercifully the whole ludicrously expensive and mismanaged railway project came to nothing, so my mother lies, among her kin, where we last put her......for the time being.

ACKNOWLEDGEMENTS

Apart from my darling wife, Louise, who is the best, most sympathetic but strictest editor in the world, I would also like to thank Coco and Emerald who read and made helpful improvements to their embarrassing father's manuscript.

Thanks also to Will and Susan Boyd, The Favours, without whom I would never have been in print.

Lastly, thanks and apologies are due to those I shared some of these episodes with, especially Ali, Johnnie, Bill and Laura.

A NOTE ON THE AUTHOR

Theo Fennell was born in Egypt, the son of an army family and spent his early years all over the world. He was sent to boarding school at five, then to Eton, York College of Art, followed by the Byam Shaw School of Art. He is the leading British jewellery and silverware designer. He lives in London with his wife, Louise, the author and screen writer. The couple have two daughters, Emerald, a writer, actor and director, and Coco, a dress designer.

His first volume of Chapters of Accidents, *I Fear for This Boy*, was published in 2022.